ABRAHAM, FATHER OF BELIEVERS

ABRAHAM

FATHER
OF BELIEVERS

ANGEL GONZALEZ

TRANSLATED BY ROBERT J. OLSEN

HERDER AND HERDER

1967
HERDER AND HERDER NEW YORK
232 Madison Avenue, New York 10016

Original edition: *Abraham, padre de los creyentes,*
Madrid, Taurus Ediciones, S.A.

Library of Congress Catalog Card Number: 67–25879
© 1967 by Herder and Herder, Inc.
Manufactured in the United States

CONTENTS

PROLOGUE

IF introductory lines serve any purpose, it is to make a book easier to read, saying something about it. Certainly, every reader will possess his own criteria, and will agree or disagree with the author's opinion about his book.

The subject of this book is Abraham, the old patriarch of the Bible.

But the book is not a biography of Abraham, nor a study of his story. If, in the course of its pages, attention is occasionally directed to the history of the era, or to geography, philology, or archeological findings, this is simply to reconstruct a visual picture that can serve as a starting point.

Abraham is not used as a pretext for relating curiosities of the past, or to create an erudite synthesis of civilizations newly unearthed, or to recollect an exotic social and religious environment. This would doubtless satisfy the tastes of our day and age. Unfortunately, however, the reader will not find much on this subject in this book.

The title of the book, *Abraham, Father of Believers,* does not indicate a synchronous study of the patriarch, finding him in his historical setting, and leaving him, adorned with interesting data, in his own era. The title announces more properly a diachronous delineation that projects the patriarch from his historical setting towards the whole history of the future, right up to our own time.

Also, it is taken for granted that this projection of Abraham to the present day can be done in only one way: the way of the *credo* and of religious experience.

The sources of this book are exclusively the traditions of the patriarch, narrated in the Bible. These traditions are a religious history.

Now ancient religious history can be approached from many points of view and with different purposes. It provides moments of interest for the historian and sociologist, the anthropologist and psychologist, as for the student of religions and the theologian, the lover of literature and the religious man.

It is probably the religious man who will derive the greatest satisfaction from this book. However, by "religious man" we do not necessarily mean a clergyman or theologian, or even a person observing certain practices or belonging to a church. The "religious man" can be anyone who believes or has difficulties in believing. It can be a person who defends religion or who persecutes it, or someone who likes an ecclesiastical system or abhors it. The only person who is not a religious man is someone who has no feelings or opinions, neither pro nor con, or who sees everything with the eyes of indifference.

In this book we are concerned with great religious themes: faith and hope, trust and prayer, election and providence, the call to a credo and the ultrasensible significance of life.

These same themes could be developed on the basis of some other biblical story, or without any story, from the simple observation of human anxieties, which some men suffer in silence while others speak openly about them. But they can certainly be formulated with reference to Abraham, once his story suggests them.

The manner in which these themes are considered in this book has nothing to do with scientific exegesis, with all the preparation which that requires. It is the caprice of the times to take pleasure in withholding the explanation of the sacred books, in the cautious tone of science, as though anyone who is not a specialist could not occasionally make better use of them. Nor have we followed the methods of the philosopher or theologian, involved as they are in the systematic formalities of their art.

8

Instead, we have considered the themes with reference to real life, weighing and feeling their implications. That is why we found it advantageous to make Abraham our starting point, and to find these themes visualized in him.

It is true that the objective interpretation of the Bible does not allow us to burden the existential aspect of the stories with our own tints and hues. For this reason we have attempted various modes of approximation to the same theme.

Each chapter is based upon a concrete motive, set forth in an episode of the story of Abraham in which a theme is incorporated. The way of approach is by *reading, reflection,* and *suggestion.*

Reading facilitates a first and spontaneous form of contact— historical, literary, or psychological—with the religious history of the patriarch. Reflection delves deeply into the real significance of the concrete episode, within the context of biblical history which sometimes emphasizes universal sentiments, and its frequent particularism should not therefore be accepted without a certain amount of irony. Suggestion, or the projection of the story towards the future, finally identifies Abraham with the believer, and indicates the implications of this identity for the religious man.

The final chapter, unlike the others, is not dependent on a visual picture, but is a consideration of the story of Abraham, or more generally, of religious history. It is a methodological reflection, as an appendix to the book, concerning the forms and ways of reading sacred history, and concretely concerning the positions of the rationalist and the believer.

The leitmotiv or guideline of the book is the theme of faith. It was faith that determined Abraham's reactions in the most varied situations. And since Abraham is the "father of believers," his experience is a lesson which will serve to guide the believer in the analogous roads and ways of his own life.

Between the sacred history which the believer accepts as belonging to himself, and his own existence, there is a communion of blessings and identical implications and commitments. If St. Paul took the title of *father* of all believers from the one whom the Jews called "our father Abraham," it is because he saw Abraham's solidarity with believers.

The way to feel this solidarity is to read his story simply, and be able to make it present. We must read the story and listen in silence to its message. No learned essay, nor the most erudite commentary, can ever take the place of the direct reading of the Bible. However much may be written about it, the only purpose is to introduce us to the reading of the Bible itself.

It is hoped that this book will serve as an introduction to the reading of the story of Abraham, and help to reveal in his religious experience the causes which define the difficult experience of the present day. If we are able to read the story of the patriarch as a living story, not only will we see him as a distinct model, but also as a human being, with whom we can feel and walk, rejoice and suffer, believe and hope.

There are, of course, more felicitous ways to actualize the figure of the patriarch. Those we have followed here are, in any case, a mode of listening in the present to the message of his ancient traditions. If, in spite of all their relativism, better reflections could be awakened in someone, the desires of the author to communicate what the story of Abraham suggested to himself, would be fully rewarded.

ABRAHAM, FATHER OF BELIEVERS

"GO FROM YOUR COUNTRY . . ."

Now the Lord said to Abram, "Go from your country and your kindred and your father's house to the land that I will show you. And I will make of you a great nation, and I will bless you, and make your name great, so that you will be a blessing. I will bless those who bless you, and him who curses you I will curse; and by you all the families of the earth shall bless themselves."

So Abram went, as the Lord had told him; and Lot went with him. Abram was seventy-five years old when he departed from Haran. And Abram took Sarai his wife, and Lot his brother's son, and all their possessions which they had gathered, and the persons that they had gotten in Haran; and they set forth to go to the land of Canaan.[1]

To a person untrained in the reading of biblical history, or unaccustomed to its style, and reading these five verses of Genesis for the first time, the episode which it relates will be almost incomprehensible. And when it is understood that this was the first encounter between God and Abraham, it may seem that the manner of speaking and responding between God and man was much too simple. It has, indeed, all the simplicity of anthropomorphic language. And when it is further realized that these few verses attempt to relate God's call to a man, for the founding of a nation, the elements of the narration must surely appear to be quite inadequate. As a matter of fact, however, the passage truly relates Abraham's vocation, and three themes become apparent: (1) Yahweh makes Himself present with a command and a promise: (2) there is the specification of the task to be

[1] Gen. 12:1–5.

13

performed in a single lifetime; (3) and finally, Abraham, who sets forth to perform the task. This is the literary setting which, in terms of theology, would be called a *vocation*.

The call of Yahweh is an imperative command. The object of the call is a nation in the germ of a promise. The response is Abraham's action in setting out to witness the birth of this nation. The movement is so rapid that the transition is hard to see. As soon as the first step was taken, the end of the first stage was already taking place. And this is because the episode was transcendent. In the history of Abraham the movement was decisive because it was the first, and because it entailed all the subsequent movements. In the departure from his native land all the later journeys were included, since the object of leaving was not the reaching of the intermediate stages, but the final goal fully attained. And of course, the use of the word *journey* does not refer to mere geographical travels. The decision to move defines and effects all the acts of life. Abraham made this decision in the present, for the present and the future. In this future, all his days are included until they lead him, if they ever do so, to the attainment of his goal.

Abraham's decision implies and at the same time confirms all of his future moves. Otherwise, the decision would have to be renewed with the same readiness at every future crossroad. But this decision explained in fact, and justified beforehand, the reason whereby the subsequent steps of the patriarch were always guided. If he had abandoned this kind of logic, he would have betrayed his first decision and there would be no other supplementary reason to explain the course he followed. Nevertheless, the scene which these verses bring to mind does not enable us even to guess at the reason for such an effective impulsion. If the initial act was so decisive, how can Abraham's strength of purpose be made comprehensible? And if these few verses truly relate the history of such a beginning, what assurance did the author possess that they constitute an authentic biographical image?

14

The literary elements seem entirely inadequate to express such a great theme: its very terms appear irreconcilable.

Yahweh speaks, commands, and promises; old Abraham starts out for Canaan, hoping to found a nation which is yet to be born of him. In the interchange of Yahweh's command and Abraham's hope, there ought to be some sense of proportion. However, none is apparent. It cannot even be guessed in what area of encounter the two characters of the story could possibly cooperate.

This was the first meeting of Yahweh and Abraham. Until then they had never been in contact at all. Yahweh had never addressed Abraham before, and Abraham had never turned to Yahweh. We are told that Abraham came from lower Mesopotamia where Yahweh was a foreign name. Abraham's clan paid homage to gods utterly unrelated to Yahweh.[2]

Abruptly, without the most elemental ritual, Yahweh addresses Abraham. Later, Yahweh will bear a name, either as *God of Abraham,* or *God of the Fathers,* and He will be known by these names, but at the moment of the first encounter He had no name to make Himself known to Abraham. The Bible records ten generations as having lived from the time of the Flood until Abraham's day, but Yahweh had never addressed any representative person of those generations. But then, quite suddenly, Yahweh speaks to Abraham without revealing His name or His deeds. And yet Abraham does not show any surprise at the command, nor does he ask for proof in order to believe the promise! He neither accepts nor refuses. He simply takes his possessions and starts on his way, thus signifying his acceptance of the command and his belief in the promise. The command refers to the present and the promise to the future. And, of course, Abraham must first believe the promise if the command is to have any meaning at all.

This kind of encounter, called a theophany, takes place only in an event of singular importance. However, perhaps no less

[2] See Gen. 31:53.

15

important than the event itself is the manner in which Abraham and Yahweh meet. A dialogue does not occur between them. Yahweh speaks with words and Abraham answers immediately with action, because no spoken answer was expected from him. Everything was motivated by Yahweh, and Abraham merely obeyed. The historian could not have chosen a better way to tell that Abraham started out for Canaan, not on his own initiative, but guided by divine inspiration. This is definitely what the author says, and most certainly what he means. The author did not need to describe how, where, or when the meeting took place. The circumstances themselves are understood to be of no importance.

The goal of the journey that Abraham undertakes is even less explicit. "Go . . . to the land that I will show you." No one knows which land Yahweh means. Abraham, however, starts out with all his belongings and finally arrives in Canaan. We learn by deduction that it was Canaan, after following the movements of the patriarch. It seems as though even Abraham was unaware of his destination until his arrival in Canaan. But perhaps the point is not whether Abraham was aware or ignorant of the destination; and possibly this question is not pertinent to the substance of the story. For this reason, the historian does not have Yahweh reveal the destination to Abraham, or for that matter to the reader either.

Abraham's action, resulting from the imprecise command of an unknown God, is simply incomprehensible. Absolutely nothing is indicated in the narrative to explain it reasonably. And anyone reading this text today will find the reasons insufficient, unless he takes into account that the characters in the story are perhaps impelled by unexplained motives or forces.

The modest literary stratagems of the author do not create a picture which, even with the use of the imagination, can form an image that approximates reality. Nevertheless, just as the imprecise word of an unknown God demands and obtains acceptance from Abraham, the entire story requires of the reader an unquestioning belief, like the belief accorded to a dogma of faith or to a fact of history which has been carefully verified.

When the critic questions the historical truth of this episode, he poses a problem of profound consequences, since in this narrative both faith and history are inseparably united.

It is evident that the writer of this brief narrative did not intend to give a mere description of human endeavor, nor the beginning sketch of Abraham's biography. This was not his style, and such an interpretation would fail to satisfy his purpose. And yet, to visualize the poignant reality that he sees in this picture, the writer had to produce a biographical frame of reference. Whether or not this frame of reference conforms to the criteria of history, it must be accepted as an integral part of the narrative, although when the historical veracity of the narrative itself is critically questioned, then the biographical frame of reference is also, of course, cast in doubt. But here is not the place to attempt any elucidation of this problem.[3] It arises because of the exigent character of the narrative. The only conclusion in this respect is that in the story exigency and strength of conviction do not draw sufficient support from the internal vigor of the events, whether narrated or implied. These happenings not only lack the convincing force to make themselves acceptable as real events, but even in an area of verisimilitude they would still present a very real problem.

Now, if the strength of conviction of the episode related cannot be found in its historical value, nor in the eloquence of its literary formulation, there must be another factor to explain Abraham's response to the call, and the acceptance of the story by the reader. The search for this factor is the first step to be taken in order to understand the vocation of Abraham, as related, as well as the rest of this story. If this particular step is achieved, the introductory episode will then be clearly understandable, and just the right point of view will have been formed so as rightly to approach the remaining traditions concerning the patriarch.

[3] In the last chapter this problem is considered more fully.

17

In accordance with the preceding observations, the theme could then be formulated, subject to the following questions: Why is it that the word of the unknown God encounters the echo of Abraham's response? And why does the story, as related, impose itself upon the reader with the exigency of absolute belief? What is the strength of this command, and what is the authority of this narrative? The answers, of course, can only be found in the literary motives of the story. These are Yahweh, Abraham, and the promise of a posterity.

Yahweh was an unknown God to Abraham. And yet, in their encounter Abraham did not even inquire of His name or His deeds or His history. As though they had always known each other, Abraham listened and accepted His commands without reserve. How can this reaction be explained? Since it cannot be explained with reference to Yahweh as an unknown God, nor from Abraham's point of view as an unknown figure, it can only be understood in the persepective of the narrator, to whom Yahweh was not an unknown God, but rather a God with a long history.

In the time of Abraham, according to the biblical sequence of events, Yahweh had not yet revealed His name to anyone. There is in Genesis a passage attributed to Enoch, even before the Flood, in which he invokes the name of Yahweh.[4] However, this passage is an insertion referring to later happenings. The Yahwist and Priestly traditions delay the revelation of the Name until the time of Moses, when the people, about to leave Egypt, demanded to know the identity of the God by whom Moses claimed to be guiding them.[5]

The God of the patriarchs is traditionally known by other names as well: the *Terror of Isaac*,[6] the *Power of Jacob*,[7] the *Rock of Israel* or the *Shaddai*[8]—meaning the mountain God,[9]

---

[4] Gen. 4:26. [5] Ex. 3:14; 6:2.
[6] Gen. 31:53. [7] Gen. 49:24.
[8] Gen. 17:1; 28:3; 35:11; 43:14; 48:3; 49:25; Ex. 6:3.
[9] See J. Starcky, *Cahiers Sionniens,* V (1951), pp. 24 ff. Another interpre-

perhaps a God derived from Haran and adapted to the moun-
tainous nature of Sinai.

In the cultural milieu of Abraham the god was chosen by
the head of the family. Therefore, Abraham's family in Mesopotamia had gods of their own.[10] From the moment that he became the head of a family, Abraham had the right to choose his
own god. And the chosen god then became a part of the family,
serving in fact as its real head. The relationship of the god with
the family that chose him was paternal or brotherly, and was
guaranteed by a covenant. This pact consolidated and confirmed
the choice for both the family and the god, and created a chain
that could not be broken, like the blood link that binds the
members of a single family together. And the chosen god became
the family's guide, warring to protect and avenge the family's
rights.

The idea of a family relationship with God is common among
Hebrews and other Semites. Among the ancient Amorrites and
the Aramaeans the family deity was called the *Lord of the House*.
The sons of the household often received theophoric names to
express the close relationship with the family's protecting god.[11]

The chosen God of Abraham could have been either accepted
or rejected by Abraham's son, although in the traditions of the
patriarchs the God of the father continues to direct the destiny
of the son. This transmission is apparent in the use of the same
familiar name that is used successively: God of Abraham, God
of Abraham and Isaac, God of Abraham, Isaac, and Jacob, and
God of the Fathers. Just as each head of a family expressly accepted the god of his ancestors, a tribe or group of confederated
tribes could recognize as its god one that was only god of a
portion of a tribe.[12]

---

tation of the name *Shaddai* can be found in N. Walker, "A New Interpretation of the Divine Name *Shaddai*," in *ZAW* 72 (1960), pp. 64–66.

[10] Josh. 24:2.

[11] See W. F. Albright, *From the Stone Age to Christianity*, New York,
1957, pp. 246 ff.

[12] Josh. 24.

In the traditions of the patriarchs, not many concessions were made to the individual family gods. Their God was the God of a tribe. Even more, He was a national God, perhaps because the traditions received their actual form when Israel was already a nation. The henotheistic concept was characteristic of Israel. Their God, however, had more limited borders than the gods of Mesopotamia and Egypt. Enlil was the god of all the earth and of all peoples. Aton, in the days of the Pharaoh Akenaton, was a universalist god, or god of the Universe. Universalism was not as ancient in Israel. Indeed, the ancient biblical traditions continued to conceive of God in terms of a family deity, even after He was known as the God of tribe and nation. But when this occurred, the one God assumed as attributes all the names which the patriarchs had once used in reference to their family gods.

In the history of Abraham, Yahweh apparently passed from a family deity to a national God. Of course, Abraham was not merely an individual head of a family or a clan, but the father and founder of a new nation, and all of the nation's history is somehow involved in himself. Yahweh is the God of the great people which the patriarch confidently expected. Accordingly, the transition is only apparent, since for the historian the whole process had already taken place. In other words, the God of whom mention is made in the story is the God of the whole nation which was already existent when the narrator wrote his account.

The Yahwist traditions pertaining to persons and themes that make up the pre-history of the nation are all impregnated with national optimism. That is why the version that has reached us is not concerned with tutelary gods, nor does it reveal the limitations of the god of each and every ancestor. In the version which is familiar to ourselves, Yahweh is the only God, and all the other names belong to Him, or describe His attributes.

The Yahweh of this synthesis is thus invested with a long history and is the author of a thousand glorious deeds of salvation. Everything that happened from *then* until *now* is attributed to Him alone.

The history of Yahweh and of the nation develop along parallel lines. When the tribes become a nation with imperial ambitions, and within their borders there are only conquered peoples subject to tribute, Yahweh becomes the God of this empire and takes precedence over the gods of the tributary peoples. However, this game is like a two-edged sword. The prophets later struggled to liberate Yahweh from subordination to the fate of the nation. When the Jewish nation suffered subjection to other peoples and their gods, Yahweh could not be said to suffer the same condition. On the contrary, Yahweh allowed it, according to the prophets, in order to punish the infidelities of His chosen people. The instrument of punishment remained under His control, and Yahweh reigned as king over all the gods, and as sovereign over all the *gôyyim*.

This was the milieu in which the real universalism of Yahweh flourished, and on this basis an authentic monotheism was defined. Israel and its God would become the center of all the world. The prophets foretold that in the eschatological future all peoples would come to Jerusalem, declaring their submission and bearing gifts for Yahweh and His people, because Yahweh is the only God, and Israel the chosen people, the first among all the nations.

In the patriarchal traditions, the theological conception had not yet evolved to this degree. Nevertheless, the God who addressed Abraham already has a long history. He was not an unknown God, but rather a God who had performed great deeds for His people. For this reason the author could picture God as giving orders and making promises, without surprising or bewildering Abraham in any way. It was not important to say where God came from or how He appeared. He spoke exteriorly, but He was not merely an impersonal force of Nature. God appeared to Abraham as a personal Being, in the manner of a man, and yet superior to him and to all that exists. That is why He could command and be instantly obeyed.

Yahweh speaks about Abraham, which means that He was not within him, as an interior voice. Neither pantheism nor mysticism has the slightest place in this story. Yahweh directs and commands the entire episode from without. And although it resembles a dialogue in the human manner, there is yet an unbridgeable chasm between Yahweh and Abraham. Yahweh speaks and His word requires obedience, or sets the characters of the story in motion. He makes promises, and there is no room for doubt that these promises will be fulfilled, for His power is known, and so likewise His fidelity.[13]

Consequently, there could be no other response for Abraham. Not a single factor in the episode arose from nothingness, neither Yahweh nor the command nor the promise. Everything was sustained by a firm foundation, which the author does not evoke, but he is obviously well aware of it.

This is why the person who reads the story of Abraham for the first time will find its literary elements inadequate. Without previous knowledge of the whole people, he cannot hope to understand the episode in its true dimensions. It is only the subsequent history that explains who the God really is that spoke suddenly to Abraham. Even Abraham could not have understood or acted, except that the Abraham of the narrative knows Yahweh through His people, having already traveled far and wide down the paths of history. The author, accordingly, did not need to make introductions. When he says "Yahweh spoke to Abraham" he is presenting the God who made Himself known through His deeds. Tradition knows His name and has experienced the vigor of His word.

The movement of the story is rapid, and it proceeds with absolute sureness. There is not a moment of foundering or fretting, nor is any step taken in an opposite direction. Attainment of the goal is already guaranteed from the very start of the journey.

[13] See Gen. 15:1; II Sam. 22:31; Is. 41:8s.

In these circumstances, the narrative requires the most complete acceptance from the reader, quite like the acceptance which Yahweh's command required from Abraham. In both cases, it is a matter of belief. To the patriarch this took the form of Yahweh's command, and to the reader it is visualized in the elements of the story. The author simply takes it for granted that neither the one nor the other could refuse complete assent.

If the reader stops at the intra-historic and "earthly" factors, he will consider the frame of reference unreal and the literary elements as being obviously insufficient. However, if that is the case, the reader will not have entered into the author's purpose, nor will he have understood the strength of the author's objective recourse. In these recourses there is the dynamic shaping of a creed. And apart from this creed the same words have a wholly different lingual meaning.

Abraham, likewise, is a new man at first sight. In the actual order of biblical traditions, everything previously written about him is simply genealogical information of sacerdotal authorship which tells us that Abraham came from Ur of the Chaldees, known at that time as Haran, and that his wife Sarai was barren.[14] Consequently, the real story of Abraham begins with the account of his vocation, which is what concerns us here.

Yahweh had barely finished speaking when the author puts Abraham on his way, without explaining who Abraham is. The reader knows nothing about his physical appearance or his human personality or moral character. Nor does he learn anything at this moment, except that Abraham was seventy-five years old when he departed from Haran and possessed a few things which he took with him. This tells us very little about Abraham.

The rabbinic midrash and the Koran, being unable to bear this silence concerning the patriarch's life and person, enriched the story with colorful tales about his childhood and his years of mature manhood. This really was an enrichment with respect

14 Gen. 11:26 ff.

23

to visualization, but in this case it constitutes a deprivation of the profundity of what was left unsaid but was meant to be felt.

For it was not for lack of time or resources that the author omitted the human and personal aspects of the patriarch. In other instances we find him lavishly filling pages with details of little importance. Abraham, in the author's opinion, had a dimension which could not be formulated by merely relating details of his life. This dimension is measurable only in the light of subsequent history.

As a historical figure Abraham was a simple nomad, owning flocks of sheep, who lived like all the nomads of his class in the borderland between the cultivated regions of the settler and the broad, open desert. He was familiar with the settler's customs and laws, and had partly assimilated them. Wherever he wandered, he took them along as part of his inheritance. The traditions of Abraham and the other patriarchs continued to reflect these customs, intermixed with the ways and customs of the Bedouin.

The nomad chronically suffers from the mirage of the city and fertile land. He dreams of the day when he will own such land himself. The normal goal of his deepest aspirations is possession of it. However, he does not want possession to change his way of life, for that would be a very rare nomadic ambition, but he dreams of richly feeding his flocks and providing his family with wealth. If something or someone promises him possession, the nomad will immediately set out on his way.

The author pictures Abraham with the promise of a posterity in the midst of a fertile land, and journeying towards it. With him he carries the few possessions accumulated in the course of a lifetime. All of this, so far, is characteristic of the nomad. Nothing is an exclusive characteristic of Abraham.

What is unique about Abraham at the moment is that new horizons have been opened to him although he is already an old man in the declining years of life. He has no children and his wife is barren and also in old age. In this condition he receives

the promise that enhances his illusion of becoming the father
of a large family, and flatters his ambition to own land which
he will not have to leave, as he left others he had once known.

Abraham's inconsiderable identity had been defined by the
condition of his family, his parental clan, and by the names of
his protecting gods. His personality was simply the concrete
realization of the family group in himself. But he loses this
personal identity as he goes beyond and away from the old
family frontiers. With nobody's protection, Abraham sets forth
on his journey, seeking a new personality that will be defined by
his own name. However, at the moment of departure all of this
still lies in the future. The author leaves him once he has set
him on his way, and the reader, for his part, cannot accompany
him since he does not know the way.

We are told that Lot, the son of his brother, also went with
Abraham. However, Lot apparently had no real connection with
Abraham, and journeying alone he went along to be the father
of other peoples. Abraham traveled alone with only his barren
wife and his meager possessions. The author builds his entire
story with these few elements.

If we insist upon having additional facts about Abraham as
a person, we will find that his name reveals a little more.
Abram, which was his original name, is a short form of Abi-
ram.[15] This is a theophoric name, also common in Babylon (*abi-
rami*) and in Egypt (*abu-reheni* and *abram*).[16] In the Semitic
dialects spoken in regions where Abraham lived, this name
means *the Father (God) is on high, exalted.*[17] In this same
milieu, a god was conceived as the father and head of a family.

15 Num. 16:1.
16 J. B. Pritchard, ed., *Ancient Near Eastern Texts Relating to the Old
Testament,* Oxford, 1950, pp. 329 *n.* 9; 242.
17 Another interpretation is "elevated with regard to the father, noble."
See W. F. Albright, in *JBL,* 1935, pp. 193 ff.; and R. de Vaux, in the *Revue
Biblique,* 1936, p. 328. But even arranging the elements of the name in
this manner, it may be theophoric as it is with the other patriarchs: *Yitzhak
(-El), Ya'aqob (-El),* in this sense, "Elevated with regard to the Father
(God)."

It means that once Abraham starts out on his journey, he will not be orphaned, for the God of his name goes with him.

Later, however, the name is lengthened to Abraham. This can be explained as a phonetic extension of the same name in a particular dialect, or as a way to write the name to assure consistency of the vowel which follows the *h*. Or it could be that the *h* is a new sound. In any case, the author neither invites nor practices this kind of philological speculation. In the spirit of popular etymologies the name is interpreted in the Abrahamitic tradition as though it were *ab-hamôn*, that is to say, as the *father of a multitude*.[18] This eloquent significance of the name absolves the author from saying any more about Abraham. The name alone says all that is necessary.

It is true that the change of name is not mentioned in the account of Abraham's vocation, but what is said about him is fully equivalent to the significance of his name. And it is the promise which he received that permitted such etymological formation. In other words, Abraham would become the father of a great people.

The name *Abraham* defines him exactly as the author desired. He is defined as a father, and for that reason all of his *raison d'être* will be found in the projection of a posterity. When the author quotes Yahweh's words, "*I will make of you a great nation,*" he condenses in a short formula everything he has to say about Abraham.

Abraham, the ancient nomad—the Abraham of secular history—would be incapable of fulfilling the function assigned to him. He would be nothing more than the unlikely recipient of unbelievable promises. But in the rather dehumanized dimension of the narrative his personality is shaped in accordance with the object in view. The author has reference to this Abraham alone; he is the only Abraham before his eyes. Accordingly, by merely naming him he speaks of a symbol, whose whole purpose and aim is in his projection towards the future. However,

[18] Gen. 17:5.

this future already possesses a long, past history for the author. That is why, from the literary point of view, Abraham is an eloquent concept from which the author can expect complete success.

This explains why the Abraham of the story does not need to ask Yahweh to reveal His name, nor distrust Yahweh's promise. He does not know from where Yahweh has come, or what He has done to make Himself present. It is enough for him to know that Yahweh has spoken. And this is what defines Abraham. He is the ancestor who received Yahweh's word concerning a posterity.

Consequently, it is not the presentation of Abraham as a private person which should matter to the author; nor is this the concern of the reader. It does not matter what Abraham did before he heard Yahweh speak. Yahweh manifested Himself to Abraham, and it is unimportant whether he actually saw or heard Yahweh, or if he only perceived Him as an imaginary communication. It is said that Yahweh spoke to Abraham, because this is the traditional theophanic form in the author's religious world.

Anecdotal reconstruction of Abraham's personal life is therefore alien to the spirit and sense of biblical history. Such reconstruction would only project into the scene a visual object that would divert the reader's attention and impair the realization of the profundity of its symbolic value. Abraham would then be a man reduced to the measure of untranscendental episodes which our imagination could conjecture. But he would no longer be the great symbol in whom the whole history and faith of a nation, which claims his fatherhood, is synthesized.

The burden of sacred history and the impulsion of faith which tradition has synthesized in the names of Yahweh and Abraham, lend to the biblical author certain resources of eloquence which other writers, with other resources, would find difficult to achieve.

The encounter of Yahweh with Abraham entailed for the

latter a withdrawal from his native land. *"Go from your country and your kindred and your father's house . . ."* What did this withdrawal mean to Abraham? Was it liberation or renunciation? In either case, did it have any effect on Abraham personally?

The midrash commentary pictures Abraham in conflict with the gods of his family and with his own kinsfolk. Terah is said to have accused his son Abraham before the god Nimrud, for having destroyed the idols. But Abraham was thrown, like Daniel's three sons, into the fiery furnace, and like them he emerged unharmed and triumphant. Haran decided in favor of his brother, who in his turn was flung into the furnace in which he died.[19] Here Abraham is seen in open conflict with his family and their little world, and separating from them consequently meant liberation.

In the biblical narration no mention is made of a liberation. On the contrary, the God of the manifestation formulates a precise command which, for Abraham, signifies an abrupt break with the past, and with his own gods and family. Moreover, it is in this one point that the author seems to be aware that he has touched upon the personal life of the patriarch. To say only one thing, he juxtaposes three terms: *your country, your kindred,* and *your father's house.* In the schematic style of the narrative, this is rather surprising. In another difficult situation it will be said to Abraham: *"Take your son, your only son Isaac, whom you love . . ."*[20] In both instances there is a graduation from less to more, from the farthest to the nearest, from the most external to the most intimate and affectionate.

It seems as though the author had a weakness for this technique in order to express the most difficult. Is this not a heavy hammering upon Abraham's human sensibility? In reality, this is the most human datum of the entire episode, or perhaps even the only datum which confers human character in some degree upon the whole story. In itself, it is rather tragic, because it im-

---

[19] *Bere'sit Rabbáh,* 38:13.   [20] Gen. 22:2; cf. infra.

plies for Abraham the break with everything he had ever known.

Is there really an element of tragedy in this separation? If we could create an imaginary situation with perfectly human characters, there would be a note of tragedy in it. But this would require us to forsake the author or go way beyond him. In the context of the episode there is nothing tragic in Yahweh's command. The whole basis of verisimilitude is found in the words: *"to the land that I will show you."*

What land is this? With this slight indication, can Abraham take the road that leads to it? On another occasion Yahweh will ask Abraham to sacrifice his own son *"upon one of the mountains of which I shall tell you."*[21] Is the author concealing the name of the place from Abraham or the reader?

The rabbinic midrash, consistently in keeping with its image of Abraham the man, esteems that the tension between the expectation and the unknown affects both the patriarch and Yahweh. Each new moment is a testing-time which Abraham must endure and overcome. Yahweh waits anxiously for a positive reply from the patriarch in order to continue his work. Abraham suffers a whole series of trials and tribulations, each requiring a new and difficult decision. Step by step, Abraham proceeds triumphantly, receiving rewards, until at last he conquers all obstacles. Until this moment, Yahweh, Abraham, and even his descendants yet to be born, have been in tension, in the drama of the unknown.[22]

It would be difficult, however, to imagine in the biblical narrative so much stress on the dependency of the entire divine plan upon the personal behavior of Abraham. When the author reproduces the words of the command he is thinking no less of the reader than of Abraham. Certainly, he is not attempting to observe Abraham live out his own drama. If he were trying to produce more dramatic effects, he would have the reader in mind.

In a literary sense, this would be using *suspense,* which would

[21] *Ibid.*   [22] *Bere'sit Rabbâh,* 39:9.

make the reader wait expectantly for a solution, and all the while it would be in the author's possession.

But the author is far from using suspense as a literary recourse. He did not apparently feel any need to use such literary effects. Either he did not know how to use them, or he rejected them. More probably, however, he did not need them, since his strength of expression and his secret of conviction are found in the pregnant vigor of his own literary elements.

Why, then, does he conceal the name of the place? Because everybody knows it! He knows it himself, because he later mentions it often. His Abraham knows it, since he starts out for it without any other indications. And the reader knows it, because it is in his actual possession. That is why there was no need to tell it. And by not saying it, the author is able to use another phrase which tells more directly the divine intervention: "*I will show you.*"

The psalmist says to Israel: "Hear, O daughter, consider, and incline your ear; forget your people and your father's house; . . . Instead of your fathers shall be your sons; you will make them princes in all the earth."[23] And to Abraham is said: "And I will make of you a great nation, and I will bless you, and make your name great, so that you will be a blessing."

It was asked of Abraham that he change one country for another, his own land for other land, one family for another, which will become his own. The change does not mean privation, since what he receives is greater than what he loses. There is consequently no loss entailed in the change, but rather a great gain. The author does not forget to mention that Abraham, on leaving, takes along as his own possession a nephew who goes with him, although he does not really belong with him, and a barren wife, together with a diminished estate of servants and cattle. His native land has not given him very much in life; it could even be said that he really possessed nothing more than the indispensable, which defines the complete person of Abraham.

[23] Ps. 45:1, 16.

Leaving his land as a poor man, Abraham will receive a whole country instead, and will become the father of a great people. The whole accent is placed upon what he will receive, and not on what he is leaving behind. The departure's only significance or importance lies in its making a new beginning possible. And from the moment of this beginning, Abraham receives everything as a pure donation. The command to leave, therefore, is not an exigency, but rather a gift.

All that is told is the work of Yahweh: it is Yahweh who speaks, commands, and promises. Abraham sets out on the journey, and the way leads to the country which Yahweh will show him. It is not really Abraham who will found a new nation; his posterity will be Yahweh's gift.

The effect of the narrative is not, therefore, in the human and personal drama of Abraham. The effect is due to the fact that in this rather pallid human picture is told the story of a work which tradition regards as the achievement of Yahweh.

If Abraham is great, it is because he was the object of a divine blessing. Yahweh made a new man of him, blessing him. And the blessing made him great, in accordance with the greatness of Yahweh's deeds.

Every blessing is efficacious, even the blessing of a man. Isaac blessed Jacob, and the blessing affected him like a physical increase, forever ineffaceable. Isaac learned that Jacob had deceived him, but in spite of this, he could not withhold his blessing. Esau received merely a small blessing which was not subtracted from that which his brother had received.[24]

The blessing anticipates and determines the story; but it could also be said that it is a way of telling it. The blessings of Jacob and Moses[25] know the character as well as the vicissitudes of each of the various tribes. In every blessing there are great days of accumulated history. And in all of them, likewise, whether latent or manifest, there is the theological plan which determines everything, assigning destinies to peoples and persons.

[24] Gen. 27:27ss.   [25] Gen. 49 and Deut. 33.

A divine blessing had already traced out the destiny of the sons of Israel in Canaan, in the curse for Cain and the blessing for Shem, right after the Flood.[26] But the greatest blessing for the sons of Israel was received by Abraham. Also, as in all the other blessings, so in this one there was a synthesis of history. The author, in speaking of Abraham, knew this posterior story of faith and visualized it, from a distance, in the patriarch.

The blessing and greatness promised to Abraham, therefore, were not anticipated destinies, but rather the telling of history. They do not so much indicate Abraham's expectations, but rather relate what the author had received. And the source in which the author found his inspiration was not the human person of Abraham, but that which the people born of him could trace back to him.

Abraham is a symbol, whose reality is to be found more in what he symbolizes than in himself. He is a sign of blessing or cursing for those who bless or curse him. The enemies of the people of Abraham have the sign of a curse in the patriarch, and he was the sign of blessing for those who were their friends.

The destiny of those who are blessed in Abraham is a destiny of blessing. This does not mean that everyone receives it again. Abraham received it for everyone and for always, as a sign. It would be enough to be born of Abraham, or be his friend, to be under the sign of his blessing. "May you be like Abraham"[27] is the same as to say, "You will be a blessing and all peoples are blessed in you."

Once more we can definitely conclude that if the story of Abraham's vocation demands absolute belief, it is not due to its historical strength or its literary power. Both are fragile and inconsistent. The vigor of the story is due to its connection with the salvific history of the people that wrote it. The author received this story mediately through sacred tradition. His position in regard to it is a position of faith. In telling the story he

[26] Gen. 9:24–27.   [27] Gen. 48:20.

is making a confession of faith, and not before strangers, but before a people that shares the same faith as his own. As a matter of fact, the people mentioned in the story are not *in fieri* in the womb of Abraham's barren wife, but existing and living in the very country towards which the patriarch starts out. Consequently, every element of the story possesses a profundity of sacred history within itself, such as no language possesses without these conditions.

The episode which we have been discussing possesses, as the story of a vocation, an important *sociological function,* first because of the environment in which it is formulated, and then with respect to everything which, in the future, is pertinent to it. And this is another reason for its effect.

From all that precedes, it can be concluded that the encounter between Yahweh and Abraham had for its sole purpose the people who would one day be born of the patriarch. Abraham and the nation are at the same time the center of attention, but not as independent subjects. More properly, they were the symbol and the symbolized. The interchange of one for the other would be perfectly valid, if it were not that the narrative would then lose its present story form. However, as far as intention is concerned, the two concepts are adequately equivalent.

Thus, if Abraham is a symbol of the nation, the God of the former is the God of the latter, and the command "Go from your country . . ." has reference to both alike. That is to say, in Abraham the vocation of the whole people is told, and in him their destiny is defined.

Among Israel's memories, there is the country of the two rivers, the place of its origin. But this is purely a memory, for with that country it has no ties whatever. Even the memory remains only in order expressly to renounce the motherland, its customs, and its gods. The actual separation from the motherland implies much more than a simple crossing of frontiers, as was done one day between Jacob and Laban.[28] It implies a destiny

[28] Gen. 31:43 ff.

entirely distinct, like that which Israel possesses in its consciousness. And this is what is defined in the narrative.

The episode overtakes this destiny in the apparent hour of its definition. The legends of Abraham comply a little with the human aspect, and picture the call in a personal setting.

There is nothing more normal than interest in the person, and particularly at such a moment. The call is an encounter, and this can only occur as a personal experience. Personal encounter with the Divine has its repercussions in the deepest center of the person, and can modify one's whole life. It is only from direct experience that all impulsion arises. The personal encounter between Abraham and Yahweh may have caused his conversion and made him set out in pursuit of his destiny.

However, a purely personal experience holds no major interest unless it transcends the limits of the individual. If it is to be shared by others it must lose individual coarseness and be depersonalized or become a symbol. This also holds true in the case of Abraham's experience.

The biblical narration does not contradict this psychological postulate, but rather confirms it. There is no mention of Abraham's conversion. Centuries after Abraham there were Israelite tribes rendering worship to other gods, and they had not yet accepted faith in Yahweh.[29]

But Abraham, as a symbol, was in no danger of bowing down to other gods. Nothing is said about his conversion, because all that is known about him is that he heard and obeyed the command of Yahweh.

This means that if there was at one time a personal experience, it was stripped of its personal significance in the pre-literary stages of history, and thus became meaningful to everyone. Tradition sanctified it and made it conformable to its own measure, so that those who received it would recognize it as pertaining to themselves. For anyone who accepts it, it is not merely a personal experience but rather a sacred occurrence of the past,

[29] Josh. 24.

which is still in effect or occurring uninterruptedly. And although Abraham was the first to have had this experience, he simply causes the visual anticipation of that which is fulfilled in his descendants. When the call of Abraham finally became part of sacred history, it had already become a collective creed. And it was in this stage of development that the author came upon it.

It would consequently be quite understandable that his descendants would have pictured him as hearing and obeying Yahweh's command, even if Abraham had adored other gods, and if he or someone after him had experienced personal conversion. That is why the gods of the patriarchs have no personality distinct from Yahweh. They lost it and became mere names or attributes of the one God. Yahweh, the God of the people, is the One who called Abraham, and chose them among all other nations to be His own people.

When the story says that Yahweh called Abraham, it means, suppressing the symbol, that He called Abraham's descendants. In this call there is a distinction which is neither physical nor geographical nor even religious. As a matter of fact, this distinction does not extend to Abraham's family in Mesopotamia, nor to Lot and the peoples to be born of him, nor to Hagar and Ishmael with their people, nor to Esau, who was born of Abraham's son. It is a distinction of voluntary election, which seeks to establish a visual center for a theological plan in history. And this distinction, of which the people are aware, is formed with precise designs in Yahweh's command to the patriarch.

Everything related in the story concerning Abraham is, so to speak, ambivalent, referring to himself and to the people, but especially the latter, because Abraham is simply a symbol of the people. St. Paul applies the same ambivalence to the Christian community, simply by extending the symbolic fatherhood of Abraham farther than what is called the posterity of the flesh. Accordingly, the disciples of the new faith share in the story of Abraham and participate in the same universalized experience.[30]

[30] Rom. 4:11–16.

And if the story is ambivalent, the call, the separation, the promise of a new country, the blessing also, directly apply to the patriarch's descendants. Each of them is someone called, chosen, and blessed by Yahweh. The gift of having been singled out from among all other nations, and the privilege of being in a land of promises, was accorded to the patriarch for all of his descendants.

It could even be said that it was much more for their sake, since they are the ones who obtained everything, and not the patriarch. Abraham's function was not to obtain anything, but rather to get everything under way. Alone, he could not accomplish such a vast undertaking, nor gather up the fruits.

Nevertheless, as far as the descendants are concerned, it was necessary that Abraham make the start, that is to say, that he be called and singled out, and set forth upon the journey. From him the history of his descendants acquires hereditary lineage, their faith possesses a point of departure, and their present existence obtains a definite significance.

This significance or sense of purpose is unequivocally defined by the story of the call. In this the people's *raison d'être* is explained, with respect to other nations and even with regard to itself. The other nations have not been called or chosen, nor have they taken upon themselves the execution of a plan which Yahweh has proposed. They live beyond the frontiers of the chosen country, and Yahweh's protection does not extend to them. They will be blessed or cursed by Yahweh, and will be considered so by His people, insofar as their behavior towards the chosen people is good or bad. They are enemies of Yahweh to the degree that they are enemies of His people, and they are enemies of His people according as they are inimical to Yahweh.[31]

[31] At first sight this way of looking upon others seems full of egolatria and injustice. The one who is called possesses every privilege, whereas the one who is not called does not have any rights at all, neither before God nor before those He has chosen. As though God spoke only the language of His chosen people, and other nations with their gods had no access to the

The sociological function of the vocation is no less important for the nation itself. By virtue of the vocation, the people are not just an unorganized agglomeration composed of independent tribes and at the mercy of personal interests. There is now only an organic nation with a unique purpose and solitary mission. All of this is foreseen and conceived from the very start. Consequently, there is no excuse for divergences (and it seems that this was a difficult conviction to instill), for the nation had only one common father, one vocation, and one goal.[32]

The episode of Abraham's vocation, for this reason, possesses a sociological function as important as one of the great traditions of soteriological history. In this can be seen an answer to the major problems that affected the people; and the fact that it has taken the form of sacred history enables it to obtain the full effect. Moreover, it could not have been otherwise, since Israel could explain nothing about itself except with reference to divine interventions. The call to Abraham was one of these, and its efficacy lies in its having been formulated with appropriate proximity and distance from the person, so that on the one hand

world of election. However, exact justice must take into account other factors. We are not concerned about an appreciation that is merely human and intra-historic, although in fact this aspect also suffers the effect of the distinction. Fundamentally, it is a matter of religious appreciation which comprises the "earthly" aspect but transcends it. Repeatedly we have been aware that this story goes beyond the personal and uses superhuman elements. The discrimination between the chosen and those who are not chosen is consequently and primarily of a religious kind. And this is typical of all creeds of a prophetic character (Israel, Judaism, Christianity, Islam), in which election is something essential. In modern terms, the discrimination would be described as "truth" and "error." Error (in this case, religious error) possesses no rights, and is the enemy of truth. When the division between the two camps becomes absolute (and this is the real and tragic human condition), the one who is supposedly elect, in possession of absolute truth, sees only error and evil in all others. But election has another aspect: the one who is chosen is a teacher of the others. If his principal standard of truth is open to all and seeks to communicate itself to other men (the missionary impulse) there will be neither egolatria nor injustice. The one that is called (whether a nation, a religion, or an individual) is not called for his own sake, but rather to teach what he has received.

[32] See the following chapter.

it possesses the vigor of history, and on the other hand the universal value which makes it directly assimilable.

The divine vocation points out a way and promises a goal, giving a purpose and reason for existence. All activity and suffering derive their explanation and justification from this fact. After existence itself, there is nothing more wonderful that can be given to the human animal.

There are whole peoples and individuals that pass through life in a state of foundering, without ever discovering a goal or a reason for existence. Their only experience is the tragic trembling of indecision. Either nobody has approached them to point out the road, or else, at some crossroad or other, they have lost the way.

The call to Abraham is a vocation which points out the way for a whole nation, skillfully guiding them towards a high goal. The guarantee of attainment is as certain for the nation as it was for Abraham, for it was the very promise of the God who one day spoke to him. And the condition of successful attainment is the same: absolute faith in the promise. Abraham started his journey with trust, and he reached his goal. The people likewise will reach their goal if they trust God with the same faith as Abraham, and continue in the same journey they have begun. Their destiny is founded upon fidelity to their vocation.

The *individual* encounters meaning for his own life within the destiny of his nation.[33] It is from the nation that he receives his vocation, and the individual owes fidelity to the nation. If he deserts, he loses his citizenship, as well as the vocation and the goal. His people abandon him and single him out as one who was unfaithful to his vocation. And he loses for himself all of the significance found in Abraham's experience, and must begin a new journey, like the patriarch himself.

Perhaps it is not easy to obliterate the impression of the first call. But possibly it is even more difficult to discover a new road. It requires a rebirth following a very hard death, and emigration

33 The word *nation* or *people* is used in this context in the religious sense.

to a new world. And life is not long enough to set out upon many different roads, nor vigorous enough to achieve many undertakings. Changing worlds in the middle of life is an act of heroism or madness. Only one who has an experience like Abraham's can hope to do it.

This does not mean that there are no other roads or other worlds. Hagar found one for her posterity which was different than Abraham's.[34] The person who abandons a particular road can discover another already prepared, or open one for himself. In any case, the sum of them all is too great for the imagination of the individual, and the precious "I" will only reach the universal goal by following one of them uniquely.

Yahweh's command to Abraham, "Go from your country . . . to the land that I will show you," indicated the destiny of a nation that would become teacher to the whole world. Abraham accepted that command as the symbol and teacher of that nation. And all that was to be taught by this pedagogy encountered, in its turn, in the story we have been discussing, the vigor of the faith with which it was finally formulated by its historiographer.

[34] See the chapter on Hagar.

THE JOURNEYS
OF ABRAHAM

Terah took Abram his son and Lot the son of Haran, his grandson, and Sarai his daughter-in-law, his son Abram's wife, and they went forth together from Ur of the Chaldeans to go into the land of Canaan; but when they came to Haran, they settled there.[1]

This was the first stage of the emigration to the Promised Land, from lower Mesopotamia to Haran, in the northeast.

Now the Lord said to Abram, "Go from your country and your kindred and your father's house to the land that I will show you."[2] And Abram took Sarai his wife, and Lot his brother's son, and all their possessions which they had gathered, and the persons that they had gotten in Haran; and they set forth to go to the land of Canaan. [And they entered into the land of Canaan.][3]

This was the second stage of the emigration in which they arrived in the land of their destination. Hereafter, Canaan is the center of the patriarch's movements.

Abram passed through the land to the place at Shechem, to the oak of Moreh.[4] At that time the Canaanites were in the land. Then the

[1] Gen. 11:31. Not all the texts that refer to Abraham's movements and travels pertain to the same tradition. If our selection of quotations does not take different sources into account, it is only in order to reproduce a more complete image of the patriarch's activities. This was attempted in the first part of the chapter. The second part lays stress upon one of the historiographer's theses, based upon the *symbolism* of the journeys. This makes the distinction of sources more important, for not all have a symbolical intention. The intention is quite clearly apparent in passages quoted from chapters twelve and thirteen of Genesis, commonly attributed to the Yahwist tradition. The chapter's thesis, therefore, is based on these.

[2] Gen. 12:1.   [3] Gen. 12:5.

[4] Gen. 12:6, see 35:4; Judg. 9:37; Deut. 11:30.

Lord appeared to Abram, and said, "To your descendants I will give this land." So he built there an altar to the Lord, who had appeared to him. Thence he removed to the mountain on the east of Bethel, and pitched his tent, with Bethel on the west and Ai on the east; and there he built an altar to the Lord and called on the name of the Lord. And Abram journeyed on, still going toward the Negeb.[5]

Now there was a famine in the land. So Abram went down to Egypt to sojourn there, for the famine was severe in the land.[6]

So Abram went up from Egypt, he and his wife, and all that he had, and Lot with him, into the Negeb. . . . And he journeyed on from the Negeb as far as Bethel, to the place where his tent had been at the beginning, between Bethel and Ai, . . .[7]

The Lord said to Abram, after Lot had separated from him, "Lift up your eyes, and look from the place where you are, northward and southward and eastward and westward; for all the land which you see I will give to you and to your descendants for ever. . . . Arise, walk through the length and the breadth of the land, for I will give it to you."

So Abram moved his tent, and came and dwelt by the oaks of Mamre, which are at Hebron: and there he built an altar to the Lord.[8]

From there Abraham journeyed toward the territory of the Negeb, and dwelt between Kadesh and Shur; and he sojourned in Gerar.[9] And Abimelech said, "Behold, my land is before you; dwell where it pleases you."[10]

Abraham planted a tamarisk tree in Beer-sheba, and called there on the name of the Lord, the Everlasting God.[11]

He [God] said, "Take your son, . . . and go to the land of Moriah, . . . On the third day Abraham lifted up his eyes and saw the place afar off.

So Abraham returned to his young men, and they arose and went together to Beer-sheba; and Abraham dwelt at Beer-sheba.[12]

Abraham breathed his last and died in a good old age, an old man and full of years, . . . Isaac and Ishmael his sons buried him in the

[5] Gen. 12:6–9.   [6] Gen. 12:10.
[7] Gen. 13, 1. 3.
[8] Gen. 13:14–15, 17–18. Mamre has been identified as *Ramat el-Khalil*, a place near the city of Hebron. The Arabs preserved this name through the centuries, with which the Koran designates Abraham, in the place mentioned. But the title "friend of Yahweh" already was given to Abraham in the Bible (see Is. 41:8).
[9] Gen. 20:1.   [10] Gen. 20:15.
[11] Gen. 21:33.   [12] Gen. 22:2, 4, 19.

41

cave of Mach-pelah, in the field of Ephron the son of Zohar the Hittite, east of Mamre, the field which Abraham purchased from the Hittites. There Abraham was buried, with Sarah his wife.[13]

The names of the places mentioned in the story of Abraham —at least in part—were discredited by critics until rather recently as being merely legendary. Today, however, they are recovering traditional esteem, now that the credentials of their millenary lineage are being produced. It is known of nearly all that they are the names of traveled highways, famous shrines, and real towns or cities that belonged to great empires.

When seen with reference to the tradition of Abraham, these places are the names of stages of a journey that filled a lifetime and covered nearly all of the Middle East: Mesopotamia, from the south to the north, along the Euphrates river; Canaan, from the north with the Aramean kingdoms of Syria, to the rugged Negeb in the south, from the Jordan to the Mediterranean coast; and finally, Egypt, the land of the fertile Nile.

The point of departure was Ur of the Chaldeans. Between the third and the second millennium before our era, Ur was an important city and kingdom to the south of Babylonia. When the inhabitants abandoned it, it was covered over by the sand. Until its great past was recently discovered, it was nothing more than a barren mound in the middle of the desert, which the Bedouins of Iraq called Mukayyar.

Abraham—we are told—set forth from Ur. But apart from the Bible story, there is nothing that attests the historicity of this first emigration. There is, however, one fact that contributes to its verisimilitude, and that is the destruction of the city by the Elamites at the beginning of the second millennium (c. 1950 B.C.). In that destruction the third royal dynasty of Ur succumbed, and a new population established itself in the city. The nomad tribes which roamed about the surrounding area could not obtain the toleration of the new occupants, and they were perhaps obliged to emigrate.

[13] Gen. 25:8–10.

42

This hypothesis does not give Abraham's emigration the character of historical fact; it makes it merely probable. The name of the Chaldeans, or Casdim, was unknown in Mesopotamia before the 11th century. This name was late in replacing the original name. The biblical story is presently found in a setting of sacerdotal authorship, and the most obvious explanation is that the writer was influenced by the name of the place as it was known to the Israelites during the Exile.

If Abraham left from Ur, his journey northward bordered the Euphrates. He passed by the great city of Babylon and arrived in Haran. The names of Haran and Nahor now evoke the memory of rich cities which flourished in the 19th and 18th centuries in the valley of Balik. And likewise there was Padam Aram, or the plain of Aram between the two rivers, in northern Mesopotamia.

When the biblical story could have occurred, all of this area belonged to the great empire of Mari. The name of its capital (Mari), was also until recently hidden beneath another mysterious mound which the natives called the Tellel Hariri.

Abraham reached the dominions of Mari, and instead of continuing his journey, he stopped there. The Amorrites were the lords of this empire, which covered all of northern Mesopotamia, from the eastern borders to those of the Hittites to the west. The last king of Mari, Zimri-Lim, ceded his empire to Hammurabi of Nineveh, after seeing his capital city fall into ruins.

The ruins of Mari held great surprises for the archeologist. Today may be seen the temples of its gods, the palace of its kings, and a library of 23,000 documents which outshines the great library of Ashurbanipal of Nineveh. The historian, in the light of these archives, has seen spread out before himself the entire first half of the second millennium. In some of these documents mention is made of nomad groups living on the borders of the empire, forever tempted to commit pillage in the regions of fertile land. Among them, the Davidum and Benjaminites seem to have been particularly disquieting. Their system of fire signals between campsites gave no repose to the harassed border guards.

Nomads of this kind are distinct from the pure Arabian Bedouin of the desert, commonly called "the camel nomads." While the latter live in the great deserts without approaching the cultivated lands, the others seek the proximity of the settled farmer, from whom they can hardly be distinguished. Their herds of sheep oblige them to move slowly, and make it impossible to cover great distances, and they must seek pasture near fertile land. The same holds true for the settled farmer.

It is perfectly understandable why the settler has little liking for the nomad, for while he maintains vigilance against the nomad's insatiable avidity, he must always count upon the scourge of his infiltrations. Consequently, it is not surprising that such negative information about the nomad has come down to us: "A weapon is his companion—he does not know submission; he eats raw meat; he never owns a house during his lifetime; and he does not bury his dead comrade."

In spite of everything, the semi-nomad assimilates the settler's culture, with whom he lives in a certain relationship. The traditions of the patriarchs, whose way of life was semi-nomadic, reflect an environment of laws and customs which can be easily identified with the codes of the great peoples of the time.

Before undertaking his journey to the land of Canaan, the patriarch lived in Haran, a well-known city of the kingdom of Mari. Rather than in the city itself, Abraham lived on its outskirts, among some group of semi-nomads, for the city itself was reserved for settled dwellers exclusively.

To what semi-nomad group did Abraham's family belong? Their ethnic identity is not easily defined. All that tradition tells us is that Abraham's descendants mention Mesopotamia, and particularly Haran,[14] on the other side of the Euphrates, as the land of their origin.[15] Their ancestors apparently were Arameans. "A wandering Aramean was my father; and he went down into

---

[14] Cf. Gen. 24:4–5; 29:4–6.   [15] Josh. 24:2.

Egypt and sojourned there, few in number; and there he became a nation, great, mighty, and populous."[16]

It is not unlikely, therefore, that Abraham's family belonged to a "proto-Aramean" group of Mesopotamia. These Arameans had acclimated themselves, from time immemorial, in the Syro-Arabian desert, in progressive contact with settled life. Some of them had begun to settle down at the beginning of the second millennium, though it is true that the Arameans appear in Mesopotamia with this name only at the end of the second millennium. Written documents in the Aramean language have not been found earlier than the 9th century. However, if the Arameans are to be identified with the Ahlamu, there were already comments about them in the 14th century, in the documents of El Amarna. Recently, it has seemed possible to trace their steps many centuries earlier, in the south of Mesopotamia.[17] In any case, the name of the Arameans in this context of biblical tradition may be understood as a retrospective projection of the name of the inhabitants occupying this region in the days when the story was written.

The *language* of the patriarchs nevertheless appears in tradition as distinct from that of their forefathers of Mesopotamia.[18] The language of the latter, Aramean, was probably formed at the beginning of the second millennium from a northwestern Semitic dialect spoken in the north of the land of the two rivers. As a crossroads of peoples, the language of this region took on elements derived from many different sources. But the patriarchs, after arriving in Canaan, encountered another language there and assimilated it. This language, so far as we know, was not very different from ancient Hebrew, with which we are familiar.

When did the patriarchs arrive in Canaan? Archeological

[16] Deut. 26:5.

[17] See P. N. Schneider, "Aram und Aramäer in der Ur III-Zeit," in *Bib.* 30 (1949), pp. 109–111; S. Moscati, "Sulle origine degli Aramei," in *Revista degli Stude or. Sc. Or. dell' Univ. di Roma,* 36 (1951), pp. 16–22; "The 'Aramean Ahlamu,'" in *JSS* 4 (1959), pp. 303–307.

[18] Gen. 31:47.

discoveries in the region of Syria and Palestine indicate that some kind of urban revolution took place between 1900 and 1700 B.C. This revolution, like others of the same kind, cannot be easily explained except as a movement of peoples occurring at that time. During the period, a very active group were known as Hapuri, Habiru, or 'Apiru, some of whom succeeded in acquiring the crown of Egypt. There has been much discussion concerning the identity of these people and the 'Ibrî or Hebrews. The etymological identity of the name seems to have been discarded. Accordingly, there is now no question of racial identity, since the name Hapiru does not designate a race, but rather an agglomeration of people of different races. The reason for calling all of them by this name is sociological. The term designates people of the same class or of an identical way of life, sharing the same destiny. In this sense, perhaps the patriarchs, as predecessors of the Hebrews, can be included.[19]

The presence of these new elements of population in Palestine and Transjordania may have resulted in the settlement of certain groups, producing the changes discovered by archeology. Groups of this kind include the Hebrew-Israelites and the Hebrews of Transjordania—Ammonites, Moabites, and Edomites—which the genealogies of the patriarchal traditions bind together in a common origin. It is unquestionable that the genealogies simplify in one person and one moment of time a very complex process which may have taken centuries to produce. Nevertheless, they clearly reflect a consciousness of ancestral relationship and they lay stress on an identity of origin.

Abraham—if we return to his tradition—followed the road of the caravans which came from the Tigris to the Jordan and the Nile. The way-stations of this road were Haran, Palmyra, Damascus, Hazor, Shechem, Jerusalem, Hebron, Beer-sheba, and Egypt. In addition to these cities, Abraham must have passed through lesser towns, each of which was an independent kingdom. At this

[19] On the present state of this question, see M. Greenberg, *The Hab/piru*, American Oriental Society, 1955.

period, Egypt controlled the region of Palestine and had representatives in all of its cities.

The unpopulated areas that separated the towns were lands belonging to no one. Here the nomads roamed freely with their flocks.

Abraham reached Shechem, the gateway of Palestine. Anyone coming from the east finally entered this city, simply by following the natural route of geography. From Shechem, another natural route and greatly used for that reason, descended from the mountains in the direction of Egypt. On this road were Bethel and Ai, and the cities previously mentioned.

These names are merely points of reference for purposes of orientation and to identify the nameless regions in between. In reality, the latter have always been of interest to the nomad, for in them he pitches his tent. These lands, belonging to nobody, lying between the towns, enable the nomad to move on at each season of the year according as his own needs and those of his flocks may require. Effective occupation gives him a kind of property ownership as long as no other group of nomads lay claim to the same land.

When drought afflicts the region of Palestine, the place of refuge has always been Egypt, the ever-green valley of the Nile. The Egyptians have always known immigrants of this kind. From the beginnings of the second millennium the figure of Semites has a place in their monuments. But this does not indicate any special liking for them. In fact, their incursions were not always peaceful nor free of ambitions. More than once they constituted a real danger for the subjects of the pharaohs.

Outside of their own country, the Egyptians knew them on the routes of trade. The caravans traveling to Hatti, Syria, or Mesopotamia rarely completed their journeys without having to cope with the nomads. When the Egyptians controlled the region, the danger was diminished by the guard-posts on the great highways. Their severe reprisals discouraged the pillagers and obtained a guarantee of security from the local kings within their respective dominions. The names which the Egyptians used to designate these nomads of Syria and Palestine all indicate ill-will and hatred: "inhabitants or wanderers of the sand, or vagabonds and vagrants of the desert."

During the third millennium the Egyptians built their "wall of the prince" to defend themselves against the Asiatics. If we are to believe a story that has come down to us from 1950 B.C., this wall was an obstacle not easy to clear. The story is recorded in a book of impressions by Sinuhe, a noble Egyptian who, involved in political intrigue at the royal court, was obliged to go into exile. One of the points of the story was the trouble he encountered in trying to get over the wall without falling into the hands of the police.

Abraham, like so many other nomads of Palestine, had to seek refuge in Egypt to elude the threat of hunger that menaced both himself and his flocks.

From Egypt he returned to the mountains of Palestine. According to the traditional story, Abraham went back over the same roads which he had traveled before, and once again crossed the country from end to end. Hope told him that some day it would all belong to himself and his descendants. For the moment, however, Abraham did not venture to go down to the coastal plain, nor to affront the Canaanites of the city. His possibilities provided no assurance of success.

Abraham's movements extended to the uncultivated parts of the mountains, but it was especially in the south, in the region of Beer-sheba, that he settled down. His traditions tell of tents, flocks, and displacements, and of struggles for possession of a well or for the usufruct of a piece of land. All of these things are elements of the semi-nomadic environment.

But in the same picture there are other colors which portray a community of patriarchs possessing a sedentary way of life. Among their herds, they had oxen and cattle. Abraham possessed flour to make a cake. Isaac planted a field in Gerar and Jacob prepared a plate of lentils. Reuben found mandrakes in the field while reaping the harvest of wheat. Joseph saw sheaves in his dream, and Jacob's sons went down into Egypt to buy grain when the harvest was poor in Palestine.[20] It is possible that the author of the story saw the patriarchs with the eyes of a sedentary, and that he was not very concerned about anachronisms. But it is perhaps more certain to suppose that the nomadism of the patriarchs was not far removed from settled life.

Before dying, Abraham succeeded in buying a cave and a field near Hebron, facing Mamre. This episode comes from the pen of the sacerdotal author, but from its vague and distant sources he gave us in detail an ancient form of contract, of which the best parallel is found in the model of the Hittite laws.[21] If the sons of Het, living in Hebron, really were Hittites, as a well-founded hypothesis now claims, the penetration of their laws and customs to the south of Palestine would not have been improbable. Moreover, these laws closely approximate the patriarchal era.

The purchase deed possesses all the strictness of legal form which the codes of the time describe, including the demarcation and description of the property and its contents, the names of the owners, the consent to the sale, and the payment in current money and witnesses. The transaction took place at the city gates, where all dealings occurred,[22] so that everyone arriving or leaving could attend and attest.

With the pretext of needing a place of sepulture to bury his dead, Abraham acquired property in the land. This place then belonged to him forever, and changed him from a stranger into an inhabitant. The journeys of many years through the land of promises was finally crowned with a symbol of its possession.

The roads which Abraham followed were open, used, and well known. He was not the first to travel over them. Many others had made the same journeys before, and would follow the same

---

[20] Gen. 12:16; 13:5; 18:7; 18:6; 26:12; 25:34; 30:14; 37:7; 42:2.
[21] See texts of *Boghazköy*, of the 14th century B.C., in *ANET*, pp. 46 ff.
[22] See Ruth 4:1–12.

highways later. There is nothing necessarily improbable, unreal, or imaginary, either in the names or in the roads, or in any of the stages of Abraham's travels. The nomads moving their flocks, the caravans of the traders, the invading armies, all follow the same route with scrupulous precision.

Anyone interested in comparing the movements of the patriarchs with the general history of the era will find at his disposal archeological and epigraphical material, linguistic and literary, in such a quantity as a historian himself could desire. In the light of these materials, the historiographical quality of the biblical traditions is enhanced, and finally produces a feeling of historical optimism which has now become general in our time.

However, just as the forest makes it difficult to see the tree, in the same way the mass of men overshadows the individual. If Abraham's wanderings were common to nomads of his era, why call him by the name of patriarch? What was there in him which pertained to himself alone? If so many nomads traveled the same roads, with the sole objective of seeking suitable pastures for their flocks, what interest is added because one of them called himself Abraham? And if nobody has written about the events and happenings of other nomads, why did Abraham have a historiographer?

The physical and historical probability of the patriarch's adventures certainly finds satisfactory support in the history of that era. But it is questionable whether with this support we will have understood very much of biblical history.

In Abraham and his journeys there is a dimension that differs from the purely historical. With or without it, the true dimension is equally valid. The Abraham of the Bible does not travel about merely to find good pasture and a safe place to pitch his tent. He is seeking the fulfillment of a promise offering far more than the ordinary nomad would obtain. There is, in fact, the faith and hope of a life which is not an end in itself, but is projected upon a long descendance.

The patriarch's journeys, as the Bible records them, are quite meaningless without this dimension. If it were not because Abraham's whole life is at stake in them, and because they have a profound significance for his descendants, Abraham would not have undertaken them, and his descendants would never refer back to them. Furthermore, without these conditions Abraham's travels would not have had a historiographer, which is tantamount to saying that they had never taken place. Their occurrence would have been merely physical, like the travels of countless other nomads. The full reality of Abraham's travels lies, therefore, in their importance to his descendants.

Most of the Abrahamitic traditions are centered in the south, in the area surrounding Beer-sheba. But Abraham's travels were not limited by frontiers of north or south, except that they covered the whole country from one end to the other. This does not mean that the patriarch was a restless or unfortunate vagabond, or that his wanderings were pointless. It was Yahweh who sent him traveling all over the land, from north to south and from the eastern frontier to the sea, to show him what would be given to his descendants. Thus the names of the places are not simply geographical, but rather the names of the historical geography of a nation. The travels symbolize or announce beforehand a future possession.

The same journeys of Abraham were soon repeated by Jacob, the patriarch who lived in the north of the country. And when the entire nation entered into possession of the Promised Land, the people occupied exactly the same places indicated by the various stages of Abraham's travels. The farthest points delineated the frontiers of the Israelite empire in the best years of its monarchy, when the frontier peoples were subjected by the empire to tribute.

Abraham traveled with a precise objective. He wanted to take possession of the land for the people who would follow him. The personal interest of the nomad was consequently diminished by his symbolical function. All of his movements pointed to the future nation. Abraham anticipated history, or rather it was posterior history that placed its foundations in him. That is why Abraham's travels had a historiographer.

There is nothing exceptional in this if we conclude that one of the fundamental themes in the tradition of Abraham (as also with regard to the other patriarchs), is the possession of the land. Apparently, the most constant theme is that of his posterity. In this it seems that all the profundity of Abraham's drama is to be found, and so it is, but in reality both the land and the posterity are inseparable.

Abraham set out in quest of a promised people within a land of promises. Both motives are presented in parallel lines, and both with the same urgency of accomplishment.

In the purely personal area, that is, while the patriarchs were still living, their aspirations had to be relatively modest, for a little clan did not need a whole country in order to establish itself. Everyone personally could play an important role within his respective group, whether in the north or south of the country. But the aspirations, modest in the beginning, grew with the need and the possibilities. According as the descendants multiplied, the demand for living space became more urgent. And both motives grew together, with the aid of the promises.

If the names of the patriarchs and their sons were eventually applied to different tribal groups, these same names were soon to serve as a key for the unification of the disunited tribes. From the earliest accounts of their history, all the predecessors of Israel proclaim the common ancestry of these groups and their common destiny. This ought to have excluded all factional sentiment. And when this history was written, the consciousness of solidarity had greatly increased, although perhaps it had not yet completely prevailed.

It was not sufficient that the awareness of unity be based upon a vague sense of common ancestry or the possible need for self-defense. There was rather need for the foundation of a common faith projected upon a common history. This also was obtained from the patriarchs.

In the name of these common and remote forefathers, the two great themes of possession of the land and a posterity were formulated, sometimes as separate themes, but at other times united.[23] In the real order, it is the second theme that precedes, since possession of the land was subject to the needs of a large population. We see why Deuteronomy centers everything in the promises of the land. At that time the people were sufficiently numerous, but possession of the land was again a matter for discussion.[24]

The figure of Abraham thus transcends the limits of the personal self, in order to put himself entirely at the service of the nation. The election, the promises, and the travels were all for the sake of the people. And because of this adaptation, Abraham does not remain within the littleness of history, which is the measure of ordinary men, but he becomes a symbol of eternal value, in a position to open all the roads which the people will have to travel.

Abraham enters into the country and takes a temporary habitation. But soon after being there he is forced to leave it to seek refuge in the fertile lands of Egypt. That was just another journey which his descendants would also have to take. The sons of Jacob went down into Egypt and stayed there for many years. Finally, they return, as Abraham returned, and once again they traveled over the same roads, to take definitive possession of them.

Abraham, therefore, simply opened up another road which, for his descendants, would last four hundred years. The important thing is to begin; repetition follows the certain and the known way. When the sons of Israel crossed the Jordan, to enter into the Promised Land, they were repeating the crossing of the Red Sea. And when they built habitations in the land, they came upon the same places which Abraham had prepared for them.

Abraham traveled over the country as a gesture of possession.

[23] Gen. 12:3, 7; 13:14–16; 15:3, 7, 18; 18:10; 22:17; 24:7; 26:3 f., 24; 28:3 f., 13–15; 32:13; 35:9–12; 46:3; 48:4, 16; 50:24.
[24] Deut. 6:18, 23; 8:1, 7; 9:5, 28.

In reality, of course, he did not possess the area he covered. His possession was merely symbolical. A nomad who had just arrived could not displace the old residents, sheltered within their walled cities. At most, he could draw near with his flocks, while his imagination dreamed.

Abraham spent all the rest of his life in the country as a foreigner, and purely as a resident alien. The sacerdotal tradition has expressed this condition very well in calling the patriarchs *gerîm,* or residents, and the land they travel over *'eretz megurîm,* or country of residence.

[God said to Abraham,] "And I will give to you, and to your descendants after you, the land of your sojournings, all the land of Canaan, for an everlasting possession; and I will be their God."[25]

And Abraham . . . said to the Hittites, "I am a stranger and a sojourner among you; give me property among you for a burying place, that I may bury my dead out of my sight."[26]

For their possessions were too great for them [Jacob and Esau] to dwell together; the land of their sojournings could not support them because of their cattle. So Esau dwelt in the hill country of Seir; Esau is Edom.[27]

Jacob dwelt in the land of his father's sojournings, in the land of Canaan.[28]

And Jacob said to Pharaoh, "The days of the years of my sojourning are a hundred and thirty years; few and evil have been the days of the years of my life, and they have not attained to the days of the years of the life of my fathers in the days of their sojourning."[29]

Abraham never succeeded in possessing the land of his travels. The Canaanites and their gods were the real lords of the country. And they remained so for a long time. "And they shall come back here in the fourth generation; for the iniquity of the Amorites is not yet complete."[30] In the meantime, the descendants of the patriarchs were mere resident aliens.

The names of places near which Abraham located—Shechem, Bethel, Hebron, Beer-sheba—were beyond the nomad's power

[25] Gen. 17:8.   [26] Gen. 23, 3. 4.
[27] Gen. 36:7–8.   [28] Gen. 37:1.
[29] Gen. 47:9.   [30] Gen. 15:16.

of attainment. They were strongholds of the Canaanites. Their gods dwelled in these places and exercised dominion over them. Like Abraham, Lot did not live in a city either. From Zoar he withdrew to the hills,[31] for the city was not his element. His descendants, the Ammonites and Moabites, still were to wait for centuries before settling in Transjordania.

But Abraham built an altar to Yahweh in the vicinity of each place. Thereby, Yahweh, like Abraham, took symbolical possession of the locations, and continued to dwell in them as a *ger,* or as an alien in the dominions of other gods, until for Him also the time was fulfilled. According to a midrash, Abraham "went from place to place, to diffuse the fragrance of his faith, and in order that his own name might be enhanced."[32] His faith brought Yahweh's name to every place, and both names were mutually enhanced and in progressive parallels.

This is still another great motive for Abraham's travels, establishing Yahweh's dominion over the gods of the land.

Centuries after Abraham, the sons of Israel in Canaan were still nomads and profoundly divided. The material possession of the country was slow and difficult, with stages of waiting and expectancy. Sometimes there were small groups that furthered the conquest. Sometimes the weakness of one group persuaded different groups to unite. And the final conquest was the work of all. But without this task undertaken together, it is possible that unity would never have prevailed.

Under the monarchy, the various groups were apparently already united. However, effective union was not the result of the new political order. (The union between Israel and Judah did not take place because of the institution of the monarchy. This union was a transitory episode resulting from the personal policy of David, and did not continue beyond Solomon.) A symbiosis of sacred traditions was necessary, welding the past experiences of each group into one history and one faith.

In view of this urgent necessity, the people finally settled

[31] Gen. 19:30. [32] *Bere'sit Rabbâh,* 39:2.

55

down, giving serious thought to their own destiny, and to what they could see around them. This reflection produced a system. There were cities they had not built, a culture which they had not created, and crops they had not planted. They were in possession of a land which, not long before, had not belonged to them. The previous inhabitants had either perished in the *herem*, or had been displaced. Some were still living in the cities, in danger of assimilation. All of this had taken place through the combined effort of these related groups, until then disunited, and by the saving intervention of their protecting God.

What relationship existed between these different groups that were finally united? And what were the relations between these groups and the conquered peoples, or between the protecting God of the former and the many gods of the latter?

They were not like the indigenous inhabitants of Canaan. Their God was not the same as the other gods. They all proceeded from a common father, who was called and chosen by a powerful God, and who traveled all over the land in obedience to God's command and in the name of his descendants. Everything which had happened thereafter was simply the fulfillment of a promise made by Yahweh to Abraham, their common father.

The people who were now in possession of the land were the people of Yahweh. He had chosen them, promising them the land, and He obtained it for them. The process was slow, for their just God would not destroy or expel the original inhabitants before letting them reach the full measure of their sinfulness.

The people of Yahweh, therefore, alone held the right to possess the country. Abraham, their father, had traveled through it and had taken possession of it for them. The Canaanites had become deserving of divine chastisement, and their own land ejected them. Those who still remained in the country had no rights of possession any longer. Either they had to leave, or else be incorporated with the people of Yahweh.

For His part, Yahweh had subjected the gods of the land. If they remained in their shrines, it was as conquered or powerless gods. No service or veneration was due to them. Yahweh took possession of the holy places from the time when He accompanied Abraham in his travels. Every site, since then, preserves the history of a manifestation of Yahweh. He had become the only lord and master. And even though some of the local gods continued to exist in the country, it was through an excess of toleration, since their sovereignty had been demolished.

Without the actual dominion of Yahweh, the people's conquest of the country would not have been complete. It is not sufficient to take a country from the power of its inhabitants; it must also be taken from the dominion of its gods. The gods are the real lords and masters, and they must be taken into account. If they cannot be conquered completely, then they must be placated, making friends of them, and seeking some form of co-existence with them. The gods which have become dominant in a particular land impregnate the area and are impregnated by it. It is no easy matter to displace them, even by deporting the inhabitants. Those who come later must accept their presence for a long while. When Assyria conquered the kingdom of the North, it had to tolerate the cult of Yahweh in Samaria in order that the life of the new occupants could be possible at all.

So the king of Assyria was told, "The nations which you have carried away and placed in the cities of Samaria do not know the law of the god of the land; therefore he has sent lions among them, . . ." Then the king of Assyria commanded, "Send there one of the priests whom you carried away thence; and let him go and dwell there, and teach them the law of the god of the land."[33]

The gods of Canaan remained for a long time in the land. History tells us how the people became accustomed to peaceful co-existence. But in principle the Canaanites and their gods were

[33] 2 Kgs. 17, 26–27. That is why the ancient conquering people opened the doors of their Pantheon to the gods of the conquered nations. The Romans provided a dignified dwelling in the capital of the empire for all of the oriental gods. But the religion of the conqueror was not always able to assimilate the conquered and expatriate gods. Rome's religion disintegrated, while new cults arose in connection with the imported gods.

conquered and the entire country now belonged to the new nation and their God.

This was a perfect realization of the trilogy: God, the nation, the land. Yahweh, the only God of His people in His land; the people in their land only for Yahweh; the whole land for Yahweh and His people.

The three motives affirmed this relationship ever since Abraham. It was Abraham who engendered the nation, traveled over the country and built altars to Yahweh in every place. The descendants of the patriarch, on entering the country gather up the fruits of that which was only a symbol and promise in him. But what they inherit is a holy history, and regarding it there could only be a position of faith. Thereafter, it is in terms of faith that its implications must also be understood, both exteriorly and interiorly.

The peoples that were not sons of Abraham, or if they were sons but not among the chosen, had no share in the promises.[34] But those who belonged to the people of the patriarch all had an equal part. Consequently, there is no tradition or history, no rights or destiny, that would be particular and exclusive to any one group. Nor was there justification for antagonism among the chosen people. For although there were tribes that continued in a nomadic condition, like those in Transjordania, while others had become settled, and even though there were idealist nomads at certain times, all this does not mean that the land did not belong to them, or that any son of Abraham had been excluded from his inheritance.

The theme of Abraham's travels, therefore, in the intention of the historiographer, has an important sociological function (especially in the 12th and 13th chapters of Genesis), which is presented as a theology. If this function is not taken into account, it would be difficult to do justice to the sense and purpose of his historical narrative. But if this justice is done, Abraham is a symbol. And as a symbol, he is different from all other nomads who

---

[34] See the last part of the preceding chapter.

traveled over the same roads without leaving any traces other than physical. That is why Abraham's travels had a historiographer.

This perspective has led us far from Abraham himself. To know his journeys, we have seen things from the point of view of his descendants. Doubtless this perspective was adequate for the purpose, since it was also the point of view of the historiographer.

But would it not be possible to consider these travels from the same point of view as the patriarch himself? Of course, we will not refer to the Abraham of critical history. We have already gone the whole way with him at the beginning of the chapter. And we encountered nothing more than an impersonal nomad who took us no farther than any other nomad of that era.

There must exist a perspective, whether real or imaginary, of the Abraham who set out in pursuit of the destiny which tradition attributes to him, that is, the personal Abraham, who began his travels with the hope of acquiring, for himself and his descendants, the places that he reached. This would certainly be the most universal undertaking of the patriarch, since it is in this path that all believers would follow him.

If Abraham was not a mere nomad, but a believer, and if he was not only a symbol, but a real person, what purpose and meaning would his travels hold for himself?

A journey has no greater purpose than that which is conferred by the goal which one hopes to attain. Thus the goal must be known before setting out on the journey, if the latter is to possess any *raison d'être* at all. In any other sense the traveler is simply a wandering vagabond or an adventurer.

Abraham's journeys were not merely a wandering from place to place, but rather they were his life itself. He had to foresee, in some sense, the goal of his life if the latter was to possess any meaning and purpose. Once he heard the command, "Go from your country ... *to the land that I will show you,*" and obeyed it, he saw an aim and end illumined in the distance. And this was his destiny. He knew enough to start out. He knew the point of departure and the goal. To abandon the former and reach the latter was his whole task.

However, if Abraham was a real and human person, he could not have found the process so simple. His own eyes, in reality, saw neither the whole road nor the goal. They saw only the concrete place in which, while traveling, he found himself to be. He lacked perspective for all the rest. Nevertheless, Abraham saw, not with his own eyes, but with those of the One who had made the promise. Through them he could see the end itself. To close his eyes and travel forward; to put all his trust in the promise, and hope; surely this was a tremendous drama for a man who had his own eyes.

One day Abraham felt himself in disharmony with his gods, his family, and his own past, as if he had had a vision, or suffered a scandal, or had been born again. On losing the sense of harmony with everything, Abraham found himself alone, helpless and without purpose. Nothing which had previously held any meaning for him continued to give a sufficient purpose to his existence. It was like being expelled from a paradise, or wakened from a dream. And it seemed as though he had suddenly appeared in an empty world, like Adam, with nobody like himself.

In this tragic awakening as an expatriate, Abraham saw nothing before him but questions. From where and to where, and why? But there was no answer. His peril was like that of a man who looks, but does not see, or who seeks and never finds. Or like a man in a most difficult situation, whose hands are unable to move.

Abraham had an inspiration. Before him lay an open road, and at the end of the road a high goal. He was like a foreigner to whom one speaks about his native land. Or like someone born before the existence of all other things, who suddenly sees a whole world arise for himself. In fact, a new world was taking shape in Abraham's mind. He needed only to make the long journey, and at the end of the journey he would recover harmony again. Abraham set out on this journey. Would he ever reach his goal?

While Abraham was traveling, all of his steps had a purpose, for they were bringing him nearer his goal. In each of his steps a little of its reality was acquired, on condition that the reality of his goal existed. If it did not exist, all of his purposeful steps would have been lost together in a single moment. Abraham traveled and traveled without seeing with his eyes more than one place in the road. There was not a single son who began calling him father. Nor was there a solitary mile in the country in which he was no longer an alien.

Abraham gave himself fully to his travels, but they returned nothing to him. Had he been mistaken ever since starting out? He continued believing in the goal before him, but it was forever receding. Abraham could not foresee his arrival nor did he know, after so much travel, whether he was even drawing near. Would it perhaps be better to turn back? But Abraham could not go back. This was the only thing about which he had no doubt. The land he had left no longer held anything for him. And would not the God who inspired him be able to carry out His work unto the end?[35]

But Abraham might also have turned to the right or the left. What would have happened if he had abandoned the original direction to follow another?

If Abraham had turned aside from the road he was traveling, he would have denied existence to the nation that was to be born of him. This nation was in the goal that could be reached in only one direction, the one the patriarch was following. If he changed his course, his posterity would be lost to view, or would be suppressed by a single gesture. But in that case Abraham would be the first to endure the loss.

If Abraham had abandoned his journey, he would have withdrawn his belief in the God who inspired him. Yahweh traveled in his company, engaging His own purposes in the travels of the

[35] See Gen. 24:5, 7.

patriarch. And if Abraham did not reach his goal, neither would Yahweh, who would then be an incapable God before the gods of the nations. If Abraham had withdrawn his faith, both would have been discredited. They shared a common task, exposed to the same judgment and the same destiny. If Abraham turned aside, nobody would have followed to place the name of Yahweh in the places which He had inspired. But then Abraham would have been untrue to himself as well.

If Abraham had abandoned his journey, he would have renounced the land that was promised to him. This land would never again exist for him. His journey towards it would no longer be more than a little episode without meaning or purpose. It would be the journey of someone gone astray, towards a goal that never acquired consistency.

If Abraham had abandoned his journey, he would have had to begin all over again, like someone possessing no past whatever. But his days were passing, and his youth was not renewed with each new day. Even if another god had inspired him, would he have had the time to begin and conclude a new journey? Would the goal of the second be easier to attain?

Certainly, a change of route would have been ill advised. It would have been a denial of his God, and of his people and his land, and of the years spent in seeking to reach them. Abraham would have been alone and without purpose again, with all of his past in complete disharmony. Everything around him would have been alien and incomprehensible. Could he have resigned himself to ending his days in this world without any purpose?

Abraham neither stopped nor turned aside. With his eyes he could see nothing of the goal, but there was the vision of desire and hope. Nothing could be verified or touched, except in waiting and believing. His hope and faith showed him the goal as truly as though he had already seen it with his own eyes. And if his goal was real, his journey had a purpose. With him went his God and his descendants together taking possession of the land.

Abraham journeyed towards his goal, believing and expectant.

When his strength was already diminishing, he saw in his tent the birth of the son of the promises. When his days were numbered, he succeeded in acquiring a bit of land in order to bury his wife Sarah. Neither she nor he was buried in alien land.

But this was all that the mortal eyes of Abraham ever saw: a son instead of a nation, and a tomb in the midst of the land.

What were Abraham's feelings when he realized that his life was nearly over? Could he say that he had reached his goal?

In his lifetime Abraham did not succeed in possessing more than a tiny part of what had been promised to him. The sum of the whole was, of course, greater than he. That which was proportionate with his measure included only the small things and experiences occurring during his travels. Making certain places known, building altars, receiving a son, and acquiring a field in order to bury his dead and for his own burial were but small realities in a journey full of high hopes. But the sum of the promises was too great to be fulfilled in his brief years.

Can one man obtain greater benefits? Tending wholly towards a numerous posterity, Abraham did not even become the head of a great clan, as happened to other patriarchs. In the presence of a numerous people, like that which Abraham was expecting, he could never have been more than a modest starting point, an individual who in this instance was the first to found a family. But if the succession met with no interruption, were not all of his future descendants united with him?

Abraham had a son who, after him, made the same journeys. The stages Abraham had made all bore his name, and when the son, in his turn, traveled the same roads, he found a remembrance of Abraham everywhere. If Abraham saw only a small sample of his posterity, it was sufficient to keep him from letting any moss grow over the roads of his travels, and to keep him moving forward until the whole promise was fulfilled.

The last day of his life was a tragic day for the patriarch. If he had not finally reached his goal in its entirety, it is only because there had not been enough time. The days of a man can never

HAGAR,
THE SLAVE WOMAN

*If each of its personages were to write it,
history would have very different versions.
But there is only one who has the privilege
of writing it.*

Yahweh chooses Abraham, and promises that he will be the father of many descendants.

Abraham sees the years passing, and at his side the son does not appear who would give continuity to his name.

Sarah, the wife of Abraham, unhappy because she is not a mother, asks the slave woman to bear a son for herself and for Abraham.

Hagar, the slave woman, keeps for herself the son born of herself and the patriarch.

Isaac, the late-born son of Sarah and Abraham, is heir to the promises of Yahweh.

Ishmael, son of the slave woman, founds a dynasty in the desert.

Sarah, the wife of Abraham, before entering into barren old age, had been unable to give the patriarch a descendant. The story reveals that Yahweh had delayed her ability to conceive.

Her barren condition was a heavy burden for her, and although being of Abraham's household, she was unable to cooperate in the building of that household. Her opprobrium was bitter, like death and nothingness. It was not only a privation of the joy of possession, but a denial of the normal purpose of her own existence.

But Sarah had a slave woman whom she had brought with her, among other possessions, when she married Abraham. According to the laws and customs of that era, this slave belonged to her completely, including all that she owned.[1] If the slave had a son, he would belong to Sarah, like the slave woman herself. (Rachel and Leah brought their maids to Jacob so that they might have children by their husband.)[2]

... Sarai said to Abram, "... go in to my maid; it may be that I shall obtain children by her."[3]

The word *bânâh* (to build) enabled the author to obtain different meanings by the use of this one word. He did this consciously and intentionally. The word means "to build, to construct," and by derivation "to found a household, a family." Sarah now had only one way to reëdify herself and build a family—by giving a son (*ben*) to Abraham. From the phonetic analogy between *ben* and *bânâh* there arises a second meaning for the verb: "to have a son." To reëdify herself, build a household, and have a son were equivalent terms for Sarah. When she brought her maid to Abraham, she was seeking everything simultaneously.

If the slave woman conceives by Abraham, the son will be Sarah's own. Through him she will be liberated from oppro-

[1] See, for example, the Code of Hammurabi. In the modern Orient similar customs can still be found. See E. W. Lane, *The Manners and Customs of the Modern Egyptians,* London, 1896, vol. I, p. 233.

[2] Gen. 30:1-6; 9-13.

[3] Gen. 16:2. The present story is found in chapters 16 and 21 of Genesis. Chapter 16 (except verses 1, 3, 15, and 16, of sacerdotal authorship) is attributed to the Yahwist tradition, while 21 is a duplicate of the same story in the tradition of the North. The second possesses less dynamism in the coloring of the narrative, but perhaps greater moral excellence. Both traditions belong to the most ancient Abrahamitic nucleus. It properly occurs between the promise of a son to Abraham and the birth of Sarah's son.

brium, like a ruin that is rebuilt. And once she has a son, the barren and useless Sarah will establish a family for Abraham.

And Abram hearkened to the voice of Sarai. . . . And he went in to Hagar, and she conceived. . . .[4]

Hagar, for her part, was nothing more than Sarah's property. Her only title was *sifhâh* or *âmâh*, which means a slave. Her whole purpose in life was to be of service to her mistress, who could also give her to Abraham.[5]

Hagar did not belong to herself, and consequently she had no possessions of her own. Her will had little significance, since she would not take a single step of her own accord. She and her works and achievements all belonged to Sarah, the mistress.

Hagar conceived by Abraham, and she felt and saw that she had conceived. When she felt the presence of the fruit of her womb, she became fully aware of her own existence. Within her a movement occurred which was the emotion of being. She began to observe herself, which she had never done before. And she saw the dimension of an existence opened towards a different future.

For the first time Hagar dared to lift her eyes and look about. And she saw Abraham, the husband of her mistress. Abraham now stayed, as never before, near Hagar. He was really within her, since what she possessed was of Abraham. And Abraham centered all his attention in Hagar, as in fertile land that belonged to him, with the emotion felt by the farmer looking over his fields.

Hagar lifted her eyes, looking and laughing at Sarah, her mistress. She had never seen her except as her mistress and as Abraham's wife. But now she realized that Sarah had nothing from the patriarch. Nor had she done anything to establish a

---

[4] Gen. 16:2, 4.

[5] The word *sifhâh*, from *safâh* (to pour, to spill), has the fundamental meaning of concubine. From the same word *mispahâh* (family or clan) is derived. The latter was formed by the chief and all of his servants. The servants belonged to the family. The word *'amâhes* means "servant" primarily, but it can also mean a concubine.

posterity for him. From that moment, the weight of subjection became lighter.

Sarah's importance was diminished in Hagar's eyes. Hagar no longer felt that she was merely the impersonal property of her mistress, and she began comparing herself with Sarah, face to face, as human beings. Before Abraham she possessed something which the mistress lacked, and her treasure belonged to him also.

Abraham, ignorant of the drama of the maternity of Sarah and Hagar, raised his eyes to heaven, in search of Yahweh. He wanted to offer Him thanks, for Yahweh had fulfilled His promise. Abraham now saw himself as a father, and began to consider the land as insufficient to contain his posterity.

Sarah had not had time to realize that she had been "reëdified" in her maid servant, nor to see that the latter was making a mother of her. Before she could give any thought to the child, she understood that Hagar no longer really belonged to her. She felt that she had lost the slave woman's respect.

Sarah's barren condition now began to be more unbearable to her. Not only had she failed to have her life reëdified, or to become a mother, but on the contrary, a son would be born to Abraham, and this son would not be hers. She was more and more aware of her own sterility, and the testimony of the pregnant slave woman made her bitter unto death.

It was Sarah who had brought the slave to Abraham, as though giving herself. And the slave woman had become threatening, with the emotion of effective possession. And Abraham? Abraham had accepted this gift from heaven and saw in the slave woman the fulfillment of all the promises. Was it not Abraham's own son who was thriving in the shadow of his tent?

Sarah could not prevent the course of things. But neither did she give up hope that Abraham would re-make her life, if she herself could do nothing about it. Sarah took a step, still remaining in her power, and reproached Abraham: "May the Lord judge

69

between you and me!",[6] which is to say, may He sustain and avenge my destiny which you have unjustly abused.

Abraham said to Sarah, "Behold, your maid is in your power; do to her as you please."[7] This was a gesture of total renunciation. It meant that Abraham was renouncing all the hope he had placed in the unborn son of the slave woman, abandoning him to whatever fate Sarah might determine. Certainly, she would not let the child become the heir. And so Abraham was alone again, with Sarah barren and old.

Hagar, abandoned to her mistress, could see no recourse but flight. Had not submission been her whole way of life? Why submit again? Had she ever before considered flight as a means of self-liberation?

Flight, in such a situation, is an act of rebellion and a form of self-assertion. Perhaps never before had she known what it means to lose something. And, of course, she had never possessed anything to defend; consequently, there had not previously been any reason to fear. To fear is to feel that something, needing defense, may be lost. And flight is a proclamation of a state of defense of that which could be lost. It is, in fact, the only form of defense for those who cannot defend themselves.

Hagar had acquired something worth defending when she became fully aware of herself as a person. The day when a slave awakes is a day of birth. Hagar had been born again, when she was suddenly aware of other life within her. It was Sarah's quest for reëdification that produced this second life, for otherwise Hagar would have passed through existence like some tiny creature that is not fully conscious of itself, not leaving a single trace or memory.

Hagar had realized that she really meant something to Abraham. And to mean something to another person is to possess the plenitude of existence. Abraham handed her over to Sarah, and Sarah oppressed her. But never again could Hagar return to her inane condition. Nothing, except death itself, could extinguish

[6] Gen. 16:5.   [7] Gen. 16:6.

her self-awareness. And not even death could suppress her significance to Abraham, which was an extension of her own life.

Hagar ran away to defend her own life and the new life within her. To live is the greatest of passions, the passion that provoked Hagar's rebellion and led her to take flight.

However, in running away, Hagar stumbled headlong into the desert. Behind her was Sarah's tent; before her, the empty desert. And Hagar took refuge in the emptiness, fleeing from the tent.

The desert seemed peaceful to her eyes, like a sleeping giant, beneath the rays of the sun. Hagar moved slowly, as though afraid to trample upon living and breathing flesh. But the desert does not sleep; nor does it live or breathe. The desert is dead. It is a lifeless part of the world that has never lived, or has died forever.

To penetrate into the desert means to perish. The desert buries both life and memory. There remains nothing but a mound of burnt sand, the peace of death and absolute silence.

To live or die—these are the two extremes, face to face, a critical moment of implacable dilemma. Seeking life, Hagar had confronted death. In Abraham's tent she had been born to a second life. And in taking flight, she had freed herself from the emptiness of slavery. But for what?

The angel of the Lord [the story continues] found her by a spring of water in the wilderness, the spring on the way to Shur. And he said, "Hagar, maid of Sarai, where have you come from and where are you going?" She said, "I am fleeing from my mistress Sarai." The angel of the Lord said to her, "Return to your mistress, and submit to her." The angel of the Lord also said to her, "I will so greatly multiply your descendants that they cannot be numbered for multitude." And the angel of the Lord said to her, "Behold, you are with child, and shall bear a son; you shall call his name Ishmael; because the Lord has given heed to your affliction. He shall be a wild ass of a man, his hand against every man and every man's hand against him; and he shall dwell over against all his kinsmen." So she called the name of the Lord who spoke to her, "Thou art a God of seeing"; for she said, "Have

I really seen God and remained alive after seeing him?" Therefore the well was called Beer-lahai-roi; it lies between Kadesh and Bered.[8]

The angel of Yahweh—indeed, Yahweh himself manifested in His angel—intervened visibly in Hagar's destiny, when Hagar had come up against death in the midst of the desert. His appearance was a sign of life, for a spring of water in the desert is the same as life. And both the angel and the spring were revealed to Hagar at the same time.

The name of Yahweh, *El Roi* (Thou art a God of seeing) and the name of the spring, *Lahai Roi,* doubtless had a particular history before being used in this story.[9] Its past history is hidden, but its meaning is simplified, for its present meaning is deduced from its function in the story. Yahweh is the God of the Vision— the One who sees and who lets Himself be seen—and the spring is the "spring of the Living Being of the apparition." Whatever the original divinity of the spring may have been, in this story the divinity is Yahweh, the God who sees and lets Himself be seen, the One who lives and who gives life.

Hagar was saved from the desert through Yahweh's appearance at the edge of the spring. Yahweh was the God of life for Hagar, as for the psalmist also.

> *My soul thirsts for God,*
> *for the living God.*
> *When shall I come and behold*
> *the face of God?*[10]
> *For with thee is the fountain of life;*
> *in thy light do we see light.*[11]
> *My heart and flesh sing for joy*
> *to the living God.*[12]

[8] Gen. 16:7–14.

[9] According to a story told in Judges 15:18–20, Lahai (from Lehi) could mean "jawbone" and Roi could be "antelope," thus the jawbone of an antelope. On the names of Yahweh in relation to the names of places, see W. F. Albright, *From the Stone Age* . . . , p. 248.

[10] Ps. 42, a.   [11] Ps. 36:9.

[12] Ps. 84:2.

Hagar received life once again in the desert. She went in search of it, and found it. The God who had given her the passion to live, also gave her life. It was given to her as she had dreamed about it in Sarah's tent, in the presence of Abraham.

Hagar again felt the movement of her son in her womb. His name—for he would have a name, and she was thinking of him as already born—would be Ishmael. God is in this name (*yišmā'ēl:* God hears) as responding to Hagar's affliction. Through Ishmael, she would be the mother of innumerable descendants.

Was this not life's greatest dimension, and the reëdification and renewal of which Hagar had dreamed? Her path through life was solemnly opened, and she could now return triumphant to Sarah's tent, to submit herself, although exalted, to her mistress again. Had she not been the first to attain the promises accorded to the patriarch?

Abraham again received into his tent the son whom he had renounced. "And Hagar bore Abram a son; and Abram called the name of his son, whom Hagar bore, Ishmael. Abram was eighty-six years old when Hagar bore Ishmael to Abram."[13]

Does not Ishmael's name mean something to Abraham also? Had Yahweh "heard" Abraham as well? Could it be this son, who was lost and then found again, who would make Abraham the father of innumerable descendants? If it were not he, then what other son would be reserved for his old age?

Sarah, however, was the mother connected with the promises made to Abraham. "The Lord visited Sarah as He had said, . . . And Sarah conceived, and bore Abraham a son in his old age . . ."[14]

Isaac was the son of Sarah and Abraham. According to other historical analogies, his complete name would be *yishāk-El,* meaning God laughs, or God shows Himself to be favorable. God responded with this favored son to the drama of Sarah and the hopes of Abraham. In him, all are contained: Sarah, Abra-

[13] Gen. 16:15–16.   [14] Gen. 21:1–2.

ham, and the awaited posterity. In the story of Abraham's household, Isaac held two principal functions. He would be Abraham's son and the father of Jacob, in whom finally the descendants would be multiplied.

Etymologically, the word *tzahâk* (to laugh) gave rise to much word-play on Isaac's name in the Abrahamitic traditions. Sarah, the first, on learning that she was going to conceive, laughed to herself, saying, "After I have grown old, and my husband is old, shall I have pleasure?"[15] And Abraham, on hearing that kings, peoples, and nations would proceed from himself and Sarah, "fell on his face and laughed, and said to himself, 'Shall a child be born to a man who is a hundred years old? Shall Sarah, who is ninety years old, bear a child?' "[16] And Sarah, after giving birth, said to herself, "God has made laughter for me; every one who hears will laugh over me."[17] And Ishmael, the son of the slave woman, laughed with Isaac.[18]

They all laughed with impunity, except Ishmael. But Sarah saw the son of Hagar the Egyptian, whom she had borne to Abraham, playing with her son Isaac. So she said to Abraham, "Cast out this slave woman with her son; for the son of this slave woman shall not be heir with my son Isaac."[19] In her maternal pride, keenly felt again and avenged, Sarah could not allow anyone to share with her son the destiny and inheritance of Abraham.

Abraham felt a father's grief. Sarah's request displeased him because of his son. But a command of Yahweh—as the story tells us—obliged him to listen to his wife. "So Abraham rose

---

[15] Gen. 18:12.   [16] Gen. 17:17.
[17] Gen. 21:6.   [18] Gen. 21:9.

[19] Gen. 21:9–10. The laws of *Nuzi* (the Hurrians, 15th century B.C.) foresee the case of a barren wife who must give her husband a woman who is capable of making him a father. If the wife then has a son of her own, the servant and her son cannot be expelled from the family or disinherited. In the event that there is no descendant at all, the adoption of a slave is possible. See Eliezer in the case of Abraham (Gen. 15:2). Precise regulations on the same subject are found in the codes of Lipit-Ishtar and Hammurabi.

74

early in the morning, and took bread and a skin of water, and gave it to Hagar, putting it on her shoulder, along with the child, and sent her away."[20]

Hagar took the road that led back to the desert, this time with a little bread, a skin of water, and the child upon her shoulder. The story repeats itself, or it is the same story. The few additional elements do not change the picture. The tragedy is the same, and so is the *dénouement.*

The mortal irony is that Hagar had returned to life. She had felt secure in life with the birth of a son and the guarantee of a promise. The son, this time born and named, and Hagar, the mother, again confronted death. Both of their lives would last only as long as the bread and water she was carrying in her hand. Soon the desert would devour them.

Without bread and without water, Hagar still traveled on, with Abraham's abandonment and Sarah's hatred operating from afar. Beneath her feet there was the sand, and the fierce sun besieged her body. She would die a slow death.

Hagar did not have the courage to watch the death of the child clinging to her body. She placed him in the shade, beneath a bush, and then she sat down a good way off, about the distance of a bowshot, waiting for doom. And the child wept.

The angel of Yahweh intervenes again. But now it is the cry of the new-born child which reached heaven. And God listened, for Ishmael's sake, "and the angel of God called to Hagar from heaven, and said to her, 'What troubles you, Hagar? Fear not; for God has heard the voice of the lad where he is. Arise, lift up the lad, and hold him fast with your hand; for I will make him a great nation.' Then God opened her eyes, and she saw a well of water; and she went, and filled the skin with water, and gave the lad a drink."[21]

This time the well was not called Lahai Roi, perhaps because the historiographer, unlike the previous one, did not know this name. But its real and symbolical function was the same. God

[20] Gen. 21:14.   [21] Gen. 21:17–19.

manifested Himself, opened Hagar's eyes, and caused her to see the fount of life. And life, which was Hagar's passion, was again a gift of God. Hagar would now live forever. The child—as the promise repeats—would become the father of a great nation.

The story, interpreted thus far as the story of Hagar, is constructed around three names: Hagar, Ishmael, and Lahai Roi, the one who flees, the one to whom God listens, and the one to whom God gives life.

Hagar's name corresponds in Arabic to the word *hyrah,* to abandon, to travel, to emigrate. In the present story Hagar appears as the mother of the Arabs; she herself claims to be of Egyptian origin, and for Ishmael's wife she chose an Egyptian woman, like herself.[22]

In later genealogies Hagar is known (together with Keturah, Abraham's other slave woman),[23] as the mother of many Arab tribes, descendants of Ishmael.[24] Late sources also mention these descendants insofar as they were in contact with the sons of Israel. Among the officials of David, reference is made to Obil the Ishmaelite, and Jaziz the Hagrite, respectively in charge of the camels and mules.[25] Also, among David's soldiers there were Hagrites, doubtless mercenaries, whom the king had hired when he was a fugitive.[26]

In Chronicles, moreover, the Hagrites (*Hagri'im*) are mentioned as tribes living in Transjordania in the time of Saul, and that the sons of Israel pushed into the desert, beyond Gilead, after having subjected them to pillage.[27] Ishmaelites and Hagrites were among the enemies of Israel, like the Edomites, Moabites, Ammonites, the Philistines, and the men of Gebal

---

[22] Gen. 16:1; 21:21. For a different meaning of Hagar's name, see R. Hartmann, "Die Namen von Petra," in *ZAW* 30 (1910), p. 146, who mentions *hagar,* a rock. This name would be attributed to the fact that the Hagrites inhabited the rocky country around Petra.

[23] Gen. 25:2–4; I Chron. 1:32s.

[24] Gen. 17:20; 25:12 ff.; I Chron. 1:29–30.

[25] I Chron. 27:30–31.   [26] I Chron. 11:38.

[27] I Chron. 5:10, 19–20.

and Tyre.[28] All of them were considered in Israel as nations that did not possess the true wisdom.[29]

The names of Hagar and Ishmael are, therefore, in late history, two key names which explain the origin of many nomadic tribes with which Israel was in contact in the course of its history.

If this connection seems to be merely a late genealogical simplification, it should be recognized that it agrees perfectly with ancient traditions. On the one hand, these tribes possessed a marked relationship with the sons of Israel, and on the other, they were enemy tribes. The story of Hagar explains both their affinity and their antagonism. It neither denies the former nor conceals the latter. All of them were descendants of Abraham, but they were not among the chosen.

This means that the story of Hagar was not written merely to perpetuate the memory of the slave woman. What, then, is Hagar's significance in the story of Abraham, independently of herself?

The story is told with primary reference to Abraham. The patriarch is the unique center of attention; all the other characters are subordinate to him. Moreover, apart from Abraham there would have been no story about them, or it would have been entirely different.

But this Abraham, to whom the other characters are subordinate, is not merely an individual human being. He is Abraham, the symbol and personification of a theme. The same historical Abraham is subordinate to him.

The theme of the story of Abraham is the choice of a man to be the father of a nation. Abraham is this father, and in him the choice was made. The God who chose him would be his own God, among all the other gods, and it is God who carries out the undertaking.

Even more than a story, it is consequently a theological plan. Both the process and the *dénouement* are determined beforehand. But this process alone could take place within history, of course.

28 Ps. 83:7.   29 Bar. 3:23.

From the intramundane perspective, men are the agents of history. But in sacred history, men are the instruments of an ordainer, whose plans have been made outside the historical process. The instruments are small, but they become great in the service of the supramundane ordainer.

Abraham, we are told, was very old, and quite beyond the capacity of engendering. And Sarah, also, was old and barren. Nevertheless, Yahweh would keep His promise. He would give youthful life in place of Abraham's moribund old age, so that life for a whole nation might come forth from them.

In this concrete point of God's plan the story of Hagar is included, as an episode which visualizes the mode of divine action with the human instrument.

The historiographer recalls ancient traditions and particular stories of men and places. And he brings them to life again, not for the mere pleasure of seeing them alive, but rather because they speak the language of his theme. The natural desire to enter into the private life and intimate reality of the characters is not simply an indiscreet curiosity, but in this case it is also contrary to the author's intention. All the apparent concessions to private drama and the personal interest of each character have no other purpose than to visualize the theme.

The reader of the story cannot easily be indifferent to the personal anguish of Abraham, who, although very old, still hoped to become the father of a great nation. The problem has no solution, except by the intervention of a *deus ex machina.* On stage there is a character, but this character provokes a conflict between two women struggling for maternity, and the solution is not a single step nearer.

In fact, Sarah, being impatient because of her barren condition, had the reasonable hope that Hagar would be able to save Abraham and herself. But Hagar kept her son, and Sarah remained childless. Her calculations had failed, insofar as they pertained to herself.

Abraham, for his part, regarded the slave woman's son as the heir who would perpetuate his name. But his calculations had also failed. Sarah demanded that he send Hagar away; and Abraham did not receive a son from either of the two women, one of them barren, the other pregnant but incompatible.

Hagar returned from the desert with her son, and Sarah finally received her own as a gift. But for Abraham, Ishmael was the first-born and therefore the heir. His planning, however, was mistaken this time also. And no matter how repugnant Sarah's demands seemed to him, heaven intervened in her favor. Abraham personally led the slave-woman and the first-born child to the edge of the desert.

Everything occurred without him and against him. Everything was Yahweh's achievement. Ishmael had been born of his flesh and young Hagar. But this was not a complete gift, as was the gift that Yahweh was to make to the patriarch. Ishmael had been born naturally and normally. The laws and customs of the land had given him to Abraham. Nevertheless, this was not the son whom Yahweh had promised to Abraham. Isaac alone was the promised son.

Isaac, who was a double gift to old age and sterility, and who was not the first-born, would be the heir, according to the divine plan. The chosen one was not the one whom nature had elected. It was not Cain or Ishmael, nor would it be Esau or Reuben. The chosen one is he whom Yahweh has expressly designated, like Isaac and Jacob and David, each in his own time and place.

Isaac, the son of so much human drama and divine concern and favor, was Abraham's only heir.

With his advent, all the others whose lives, until that moment, had revolved around the patriarch as his possible heirs, now leave the stage. These included Eliezer, the Aramean servant from Damascus,[30] Lot, contaminated by the customs of Sodom,[31]

[30] Gen. 15:2.
[31] Gen. 19:30 ff. Although the author does not pass judgment, he does not conceal his ironical intention with regard to the descendants of Lot's daughters.

and Ishmael, his first-born son. With them, so many other nations, whose respective origins these names evoke, were excluded from the ranks of the Chosen People. The election was not influenced by the preferences of nature. It allowed for the interplay of personal factors, but its decision was marked beforehand.

Note how the inherent drama of the story is weakened and the characters are depersonalized, when they enter actively into the service of the central theme. The historiographer has no intention of setting forth a merely human drama, but rather a divine drama, composed of little stories about men. Each character has his own role, and when he has played it he leaves the stage. It does not matter what happens to him behind the scenes. The only thing that matters is that he has performed his part.

From the individual and human point of view, this kind of story seems rather cruel with regard to its characters. But that is the ordinary fate of secondary characters in any drama. They are called to the stage for a moment, only to recite their part and leave, without any other major purpose. And if they have no greater significance personally, it is because no central role is possible for them.

Hagar, as far as she personally was concerned, would never have taken part in this story. The humanism of the story brought her out of the emptiness and silence of her existence, and opened up another road to her. But the author could do no more for her, since his central theme imposed itself upon him with an absolute demand, and did not allow him to be merciful.

It is the story's end and purpose that is important, no matter how the characters perform, provided only that Yahweh fulfills His promises. The characters that intervene along the way reveal their joy and suffering, and the reader may rejoice with them or sympathize. But their presence in the general action is merely functional, like little human pawns in the great drama. The author is not being cruel when he abandons them, for above himself there is the imperative of his central theme.

When the heir was born, Hagar was led out into the desert. And there—according to the promise—she would become the mother of a multitude of descendants. This future greatness, insofar as it was promised within the framework of this story, was not, however, offered to Hagar for her own sake, but rather because her son was Abraham's seed.[32] However, Hagar was the mother, and in the desert she was to keep this greatness for herself.

The intentional end and purpose of the story, in spite of the fact that all of the characters are subordinate to him, is not Abraham either. Beyond him is the heir whom he awaited, and to whom he owed his whole reason for existence. But not even Isaac is the end and goal, since it was a numerous posterity that was promised to Abraham. Abraham's vocation and Isaac's election were not meant to be for their exclusive advantage, but rather for the whole nation to be born of them. Abraham is a symbol, and Isaac a beginning. The plenitude of both is found in the people, called and chosen in them.

Abraham and Isaac enter the story because of service to their nation. If Abraham was great and if Isaac was preferred, and if the favor of paternity for the father was extraordinary, and the favor of inheritance for the son exceptional, it was only for the sake of the nation that this was so. Everything that Yahweh did for them both was done for their descendants, who, definitely, became the called and chosen people among all other nations.

The secondary characters, in the last analysis, were also serving the Chosen People. If they were not serving them as slaves, they served by proclaiming their election, since they themselves had not been chosen.

Beyond Hagar and Sarah there is, in concept, a numerous posterity. Sarah's descendants are the Chosen People, as she herself had been chosen. But Hagar's descendants are a rejected people, as she herself had been. The former will live in "a land of milk and honey," while the latter pitch their tents in the

---

[32] Gen. 21:13.

desert. Sarah's descendants will enjoy the favors and privileges accorded by the God who performs wondrous things. Hagar's descendants will be outside the scope of His special care.

Is this preference unjust? This is a form of speaking in the terminology of election. The history of the Chosen People is full of preferences of this kind. Election is manifested in terms of taking and excluding, salvation and perdition, dwelling in a fertile land or moving out into the desert. If Jacob is preferred, Esau is detested; and if the former obtains a blessing, the latter loses it. If Israel was called and received a country, Edom, Moab, Ammon, the Ishmaelites, and the Hagrites were driven back into the barren plains.

The destiny of every tribe and people is marked out as a blessing or a curse from the time of their original forefathers. There is no more revealing sign to know the place of a people or a group in the plan of election than a little oracle received by their ancestors.

> *Two nations are in your womb,*
> *and two peoples, born of you, shall be divided;*
> *the one shall be stronger than the other,*
> *the elder shall serve the younger.*[33]

Here we see the destiny of two peoples that were brothers and enemies, a destiny outlined while in the womb of their common mother, Rebekah, the mother of Jacob and Esau. The God who made the promise, or who foretold the destiny, was still engaged in the fulfillment of His word.

The promises of Sarah and those of Hagar forever establish the destiny of their descendants. Those who were not chosen, even if they were the first to be born, will serve the younger, making the election of the latter all the more obvious. The promises are a historiographical recourse, simplifying all of the ulterior process. Every character thus receives his part to play, but remains definitely subordinate to the plan of election.

[33] Gen. 25:23.

82

The story-teller cannot cover all of its aspects, persons, and interests. Nor can he let each of his characters occupy the center of the stage. The center is one and the story is related from that central point. Sacred history is the history of election, and it is the elect that occupy the center.

When the sons of Abraham have lived through long stages of history, perhaps they will feel that this discrimination is unjust. But if the solidarity of mankind is real, all men will share in the blessings granted first to one of their brothers.

Human history gives evidence that no other way would have been possible. Millenniums passed before man would call other men his "brothers." And if this achievement was difficult, how much more difficult and still remote to make human brotherhood really effective in our modern world. God has always encountered obstacles in His effort to be recognized as the universal God of all men everywhere. But if God is great enough to unite all men and all things under His dominion, men are slow to acknowledge this greatness. And if God is the father of all nations, this does not make brotherhood between them any easier.

A small nation with a national God—this provided the elements of a doctrine for the whole world. From this humble beginning the process advanced slowly towards the universal. No other course would have been possible. The summit could only be reached by slow climbing, following ordinary trails, while occasionally suffering long delays. Human society still has not recognized all the rights which nature grants to every man. This elemental acquisition is still in the future. How, then, could man have reached in one stage the glorious summit of human brotherhood, with a universal God as the father of all?

In the Chosen People there was a pedagogical function. The peoples and religions inheriting from Israel have also assumed this function. Any of them would be unfaithful to this inheritance if there were an attempt to keep for itself the prerogatives of election, thus closing the doors to human brotherhood and confining the fatherhood of God within narrow frontiers.

Hagar is a symbol of what it means to live outside the "chosen" land. But in spite of everything she goes on living. Her sons also live, although far from Isaac's descendants, out in the desert. All of them survive their own drama, as well as the drama in which others were preferred to them in a determined theology.

Their father was a fierce man, like a wild beast. The sons, "like wild asses in the desert . . . go forth to their toil, seeking prey in the wilderness as food for their children."[34]

> *Who has let the wild ass go free?*
> *Who has loosed the bonds of the swift ass,*
> *to whom I have given the steppe for his home,*
> *and the salt land for his dwelling place?*
> *He scorns the tumult of the city;*
> *he hears not the shouts of the driver.*
> *He ranges the mountains as his pasture,*
> *and he searches after every green thing.*[35]

Ishmael, the "expert with the bow,"[36] dwelled over against all his kinsmen, with "his hand against every man and every man's hand against him"[37]; his sons lived in freedom and as vagabonds, like all the sons of the desert.

However, the land and the way of life were of no importance. Hagar went on living in her descendants, as Sarah lived in hers, the former in the scorched steppe, the latter in the favored land. What really matters is to live. And to live is not as simple as passing over a field. To live is a continual surmounting of deadly obstacles.

When Hagar awoke to an awareness of herself, she emerged from the condition of a slave. When she was about to die in the desert, the Angel of Yahweh restored her to life. And when it seemed as though she would be lost in the pragmatic process of the story, a new road in life was opened to her. Her destiny was to serve the descendants of Sarah, but for herself, in order to live,

---

[34] Job 24:5.
[36] Gen. 21:20.
[35] Job 39:5–8.
[37] Gen. 16:12.

her own little story was sufficient. Her passionate desire to live forever was surely the same as Abraham's and Sarah's.

Yahweh renewed his promises in favor of Isaac. The Chosen People would be born of him. And the land which this people occupied would be the land of election. The frontiers of the nation would mark the limits of Yahweh's land also. Does this mean that Yahweh would not go further and beyond the flocks of the sons of Isaac?

In any case, the God who listened to Hagar's affliction and Ishmael's weeping was the same Yahweh, the God of Abraham and of Isaac. He it was who promised her that she would be the mother of a great people, and He fulfilled His promise. Hagar went out into the desert, far beyond the limits of Yahweh's land. Did Yahweh go with Hagar, or did she find another God in the desert? And if Yahweh showed preference for another people, and reserved a country for their homeland, what could He reserve for her?

Hagar knew no other God than the One she learned to know while living with Abraham's clan. And it was the same God who accompanied her into the desert. Hagar could not feel that Yahweh had rejected her. But did she realize that she was not the chosen one? Had she not received from nothingness a new life, a name, and a posterity?

When she set out on her journey, Hagar abandoned Abraham's clan, which was a center of election. But was not the clan which she herself founded still another center of election? If the descendants of Sarah inherited the promises, and continued to be the center of the story, may we not say that Hagar also received promises and had a little story of her own in which her descendants play the central role? Do we not find two parallel spheres of election?

Yahweh, the God of Abraham, is the God of both spheres, although the peoples and lands, the names and stories are different. There are as many stories of God's salvation as there are clans or peoples who have a history of election. In each of them it is the same God who chooses and promises, accompanies and defends.

The experience of an encounter with God begins in the individual and is transmitted to the group. God is present in the historical process and lets the encounter with Himself take place. And through its own historical experience each group encounters Him. The universal God diminishes Himself in the history of men whenever they are unable to conceive of Him and of life without frontiers.

Ishmael had no share in Isaac's election, but he had his own. Both were sons of Abraham, although one remained in Abraham's tent while the other fled to the desert.

The same God of Abraham chose the two of them in order that each might be the father of a great nation. Both were sons of the same benevolence. Which of the two could say that he alone had been chosen? Which of them could feel rejected? If one of them was given the central role in his particular story, was not the other one the center of his own?

Hagar is the symbol of life for anyone outside of a human council, a symbol of hope for anyone suffering from suppression in discord. Human councils are little stories without parts for everyone. Nevertheless, all men share as brothers in the great story of mankind. The universal God directing it recognizes no limits of races or frontiers, churches or theologies.

Abraham, the old patriarch, holds his arms open to the sons of Sarah and those of Hagar, for all are equally his own. And he holds his arms open to the sons of his faith, who are all the believers.

THE PRAYER FOR SODOM

*"If you want to possess the world, there can
be no justice, and if it be justice that you
want, you cannot have the world. You cling
to both extremes: you want both the world
and justice. But if you do not yield a little,
the world cannot subsist."*[1]

And Abraham went early in the morning to the place where he had
stood before the Lord; and he looked down toward Sodom and
Gomorrah and toward all the land of the valley, and beheld, and lo,
the smoke of the land went up like the smoke of a furnace.[2]

He had passed by the same place other times, walking behind
his nomadic flocks, and had seen rich cities and green fields, made
to tempt the cupidity of the mountain nomad. When Lot had to
separate from Abraham because of quarrels between their shep-
herds, he had chosen for himself and his flocks this level land
that was well watered everywhere "like the garden of the Lord,
like the land of Egypt."[3]

Now a heavy pall of smoke covered the whole region, making
it completely inaccessible to the Bedouin, even with his eyes. And
Abraham knew that beneath the silent smoke there was nothing
left but the brutal destruction of a catastrophe.

There were, in fact, no survivors, not even one dragging his
burnt body or his terrified mind. Not a man, animal, or insect

[1] *Bere'sit Rabbâh,* 49:9.
[2] Gen. 19:17–28; the entire theme in Chapters 18 and 19.
[3] Gen. 13:10; see Gen. 2:8; Ezek. 28:13; 31:8–9.

emerged in wounded condition from the ruins; not a tree, plant, or blade of grass had not been shaken by the final quiver. There was only death.

Abraham had risen early with the presentiment of tragedy, and he rushed to the place with hurried steps. Perhaps he felt an urge to contradict or deny the tragic presentiment and assure himself that the cities were in fact still standing, or perhaps he hoped to delay at the last moment the signal of extermination, as if his vigorous pace somehow lent him strength for this purpose.

Surely it was inconceivable that Yahweh had been unjust. Abraham had no doubt about this. In the event of general death, Lot must have saved himself. No just man could have been buried beneath the same ruins with the sinner. But Abraham's anxiety extended even further. If only there had been ten just men, the cities would have been spared; if his prayer had been heard with favor; and if Yahweh had turned away from His wrath.

Abraham reached the high place and saw the cloud of smoke, feeling great despair. He felt a sudden shiver of weakness and impotence. The heavy suspicions of the night before had not suggested such a hideous picture. The veil of smoke covered four dead cities, and in their ashes there was also something of his own, a prayer of hope that was also dead.

Everything had happened between the time of his waking and the moment when he arrived, breathless, at the place of lookout.

The sun had risen on the earth when Lot came to Zoar. Then the Lord rained on Sodom and Gomorrah brimstone and fire from the Lord out of heaven; and he overthrew those cities, and all the valley, and all the inhabitants of the cities, and what grew on the ground.[4]

On the western shore of the Dead Sea, to the south, there is today a name, Sodom, that evokes the place of the catastrophe. Success has not crowned the efforts of archeologists seeking the buried cities, yet the irregular structure and the recent geological formation indicate an abnormal region where disturbances are likely to occur.

[4] Gen. 19:23–25.

On the eastern shore of the Dead Sea, opposite Sodom, there is a small village called Tzefi. More than one person has imagined that Zoar, the town which Lot chose for refuge, once stood here. It is a fertile region, in the midst of a saline area, as though enjoying some privileges of nature, in contrast with the ruggedness of the desert and the reddish mountains of Edom. In the same area there are the remains of a dwelling of the Roman era which an earthquake, during the same era, delivered over to the waters of the Dead Sea. Later, during the Byzantine period, the place had new inhabitants, and today it survives in the aforementioned village.

On the hills of Sodom there are huge blocks of saline stone and, here and there, rocks of fantastic shape and form, stimulating the popular imagination to tell again the episode of Lot's wife.

This region, so unfortunate geologically, has been inhabited since earliest times. Caravans of merchants passed through it, traveling from Edom to the Negeb, and from Mesopotamia to Egypt. In its ancient local traditions the memory of a remote catastrophe has been preserved, and finally found its place in the traditions of Abraham.

Deuteronomy evokes the episode of Sodom with the usual formulas of etiology,[5] and draws a lesson from it for the people of the Covenant.

And the generation to come, your children who rise up after you, and the foreigner who comes from a far land, would say, when they see the afflictions of that land and the sicknesses with which the Lord has made it sick—the whole land brimstone and salt, and a burnt-out waste, unsown, and growing nothing, where no grass can sprout, an overthrow like that of Sodom and Gomorrah, Admah and Zeboiim, which the Lord overthrew in his anger and wrath—yea, all the nations would say, "Why has the Lord done thus to this land? What means the heat

[5] *Etiology* is the explanation of a phenomenon, a fact or deed, a name, by its causes. A ruin, a pile of stones, an altar, the name of a place or a person, are things requiring an explanation of their origin and purpose. The etiological explanation provides the answer, sometimes with the data of an historical tradition, and at other times with stories created by the imagination. The purpose of the explanation is usually pragmatic.

of this great anger?" Then men would say, "It is because they forsook the covenant of the Lord, the God of their fathers, . . ."[6]

In the present story, etiological explanations of this kind are abundant, especially with regard to names, as for instance, Isaac, Zoar, Moab, and Ammon.[7]

The episode of Lot's wife seems like a story purposely contrived to explain the strange saline rocks in human form which are seen everywhere in the region. And perhaps the destruction of the cities also concords with the existence of some ancient ruin in this bituminous and shifting soil.

If this point of view does not support the historical reality of the tradition, it must be remembered that historical reality is not the only form of reality, nor is it the most important. The whole narrative has its greatest reality in its doctrinal and pragmatic purpose. Sodom serves to visualize an episode in Yahweh's revelation to the people of Israel. It is an aspect of their election in Abraham, their first father.

Why does Abraham intercede for Sodom? What enabled and impelled him to undertake such mediation?

As soon as Yahweh and Abraham knew each other, Abraham, according to the story, entered into Yahweh's confidence and learned to speak with Him, just as a man speaks with his friend. Yahweh, for His part, granted exceptional favors to Abraham. Yahweh said to Abimelech, "Now then restore the man's wife; for he is a prophet, and he will pray for you, and you shall live."[8] And Abimelech survived, because of Abraham's intercession. The psalmist said of him, as of other prophets, "Touch not my anointed ones, do my prophets no harm."[9]

Why was Abraham called a prophet? Before all else, the term means a mediator. Moses, the greatest of the prophets, was able to restrain Yahweh's wrath in the moment of punishment. The

6 Deut. 29:22–25.
7 Respectively from *tzahak*, to laugh (Gen. 18:13, 15; 17:17; 21:6); *mitz'ar*, insignificance, a small thing (Gen. 19:20); *me'ab*, conceived of the father (Gen. 19:37); *ben' ammi*, son of my kinsman (Gen. 19:38).
8 Gen. 20:7.   9 Ps. 105:15.

90

terrible force of the numinous was neutralized and became harmless through his mediation. "You speak to us, and we will hear; but let not God speak to us, lest we die."[10] To speak in Yahweh's name and place, like the prophet, is to transform the numinous from something mysterious into someone benevolent.

And the people came to Moses, and said, "We have sinned, for we have spoken against the Lord and against you; pray to the Lord, that he take away the serpents from us.[11] . . . and when the Lord heard it, his anger was kindled, and the fire of the Lord burned among them, . . . Then the people cried to Moses; and Moses prayed to the Lord, and the fire abated.[12]

Abraham, who was also called a prophet, interceded in the same way. Before the messengers of doom had reached Sodom, Yahweh said, "Shall I hide from Abraham what I am about to do. . . . ?"[13] and then Yahweh made known to Abraham the outcry of Sodom's sins, and His intention to destroy it. The terrible numinous was about to enter into direct contact with Sodom, but first this was revealed to Abraham.

And Abraham stood up before God, between Yahweh and Sodom, and interceded.

"Wilt thou indeed destroy the righteous with the wicked? Suppose there are fifty righteous within the city; wilt thou then destroy the place and not spare it for the fifty righteous who are in it? Far be it from thee to do such a thing, to slay the righteous with the wicked, so that the righteous fare as the wicked! Far be that from thee! Shall not the Judge of all the earth do right?" And the Lord said, "If I find at Sodom fifty righteous in the city, I will spare the whole place for their sake." Abraham answered, "Behold, I have taken upon myself to speak to the Lord, I who am but dust and ashes. Suppose five of the fifty righteous are lacking? Wilt thou destroy the whole city for lack of five?" And he said, "I will not destroy it if I find forty-five there." Again he spoke to him, and said, "Suppose forty are found there." He answered, "For the sake of forty I will not do it." Then he said, "Oh let not the Lord be angry, and I will speak. Suppose thirty are found there." He answered, "I will not do it, if I find thirty there." He said,

[10] Ex. 20:19.
[11] Num. 21:7.
[12] Num. 11:1, 2.
[13] Gen. 18:17.

"Behold, I have taken upon myself to speak to the Lord. Suppose twenty are found there." He answered, "For the sake of twenty I will not destroy it." Then he said, "Oh let not the Lord be angry, and I will speak again but this once. Suppose ten are found there." He answered, "For the sake of ten I will not destroy it." And the Lord went his way, when he had finished speaking to Abraham; and Abraham returned to his place.[14]

Abraham went into his tent at nightfall, and fell asleep hoping that there were ten righteous men keeping vigil over the threatened cities. He had done what was in his power to do. He had bargained with Yahweh down to the minimum number. And he did not believe that he could do any more.

Abraham's prayer, along with the number of righteous men, counted in favor of the cities. And Yahweh's justice had also been placed in the balance. If Yahweh caused the righteous to perish together with the wicked, Abraham's intercession would perish, and Yahweh, as the just Judge of all the earth, would perish too.

Abraham felt very hopeful. The life of the cities was guaranteed by Yahweh's justice, by his own intercession, and by the vigilance of ten righteous men.

At daybreak, however, Abraham arose with the presentiment of tragedy. In reality, only the ten righteous men could save the cities. If they did not exist, Yahweh's justice would be wholly free, and his prayer would perish with the cities. Had there been ten righteous men?

Yahweh's messengers arrived in Sodom towards evening to ascertain the cause of the outcry that had risen to heaven. Lot met them, prostrating himself, face downward, and urged them to enter his house so that they would not be left to the dereliction of the street. They washed their feet and spent the night, and early in the morning they went their way.

But before they lay down, the men of the city, the men of

[14] Gen. 18:23–33.

Sodom, both young and old, all the people to the last man, surrounded the house; and they called to Lot, "Where are the men who came to you tonight? Bring them out to us, that we may know them."[15]

Tradition later limited Sodom's sin to unnatural vice. In fact, sacerdotal law declared it to be abominable among sins, and punished it with death.[16]

However, the first and greatest sin of Sodom was the violation of hospitality. Nomadic society sustains and defends itself by two principal laws: hospitality and the blood vengeance. When the individual leaves the sphere of protection of his own clan, the clan defends him against enemies and strangers, inclement nature, and all other external dangers.[17] The blood vengeance maintains order within society. In Israel, even after general settlement, these laws of the desert remained in force.

Lot was hospitable to the strangers, bringing them from the dereliction and disorder of the street into the shelter of his house. The inhabitants of Sodom violated hospitality, for so long as a stranger is someone's guest he is inviolable. This was the great sin of Sodom.

A similar story tells how all the tribes of Israel took vengeance against the Benjaminites when Gibeah, one of the cities of Benjamin, violated hospitality in a stranger. A Levite of Ephraim[18] had arrived with his concubine to spend the night in the city. An elderly Ephraimite living there had found him in the market place and gave him lodging. The men of the town gathered to demand that the visitor be handed over to them.

And the man, the master of the house, went out to them and said to them, "No, my brethren, do not act so wickedly; seeing that this man has come into my house, do not do this vile thing.[19]

15 Gen. 19:4s.   16 Lev. 18:22; 20:13.
17 *Cain,* on being expelled from his clan, was especially afraid of this danger (see Gen. 4:14).
18 Judg. 19:20.   19 Judg. 19:23.

The men of Gibeah violated hospitality, and all the tribes of Israel took vengeance, until nearly all of the Benjaminite tribe was exterminated.

As in Gibeah, so also in Sodom, it was a resident alien—*ger*—who exercised hospitality. And the punishment that followed was in both cases the most severe, because of the violation of this fundamental law.

Abraham arrived at the high place and found that his prayer was dead among the ashes of Sodom. But Yahweh's justice had been vindicated. For evidence, the sinful cities were there in ruins, and Lot without injury in Zoar. Not one righteous man had perished, because there were no righteous men. From the youngest to the oldest, as the story insists, all had violated hospitality.

But Abraham's prayer had perished also. He had not prayed for Lot, nor for those who were righteous. Instead, because of them, he had prayed for all the cities. Yahweh had not taken Abraham's prayer into account, to act favorably upon it.

Lot, the only righteous man in Sodom, had saved himself, so that in himself the justice of Yahweh might be scrupulously preserved. Moreover, Lot had saved the town of Zoar, which was also destined to perish. The forces of extermination spared this town on the edge of the general ruin for the sake of this one righteous man.

Lot had asked for the salvation of Zoar, not because of its inhabitants, but for his own sake. On the pretext that it was merely a "little" place, Lot persuaded the messengers and obtained his request. Was not his prayer a selfish whim? Why was Lot able to persuade Yahweh to do this small and selfish thing, while Abraham, who interceded for four cities, accomplished nothing? If Yahweh cooperated with Lot even beyond His justice, why was there no other response to Abraham's request?

Sodom had sinned and the price had to be paid. Its sin was like some objective thing that moved over the land and contaminated it, filling it with infection like some contagious disease. Sodom was like a criminal, stoned to death, whose tomb is then covered over with rocks, so that his spirit cannot come forth to contaminate the country again. And Sodom also had to be totally destroyed and disappear, buried beneath its ruins, so that its evil could never again arise.

The sins of Sodom "cried out to heaven" like Abel's blood, poured out upon the ground.[20] The land itself lifted up its cry because it could not bear within itself the unavenged blood. Sodom had to die. Nevertheless, Abraham prayed for Sodom. His prayer affirmed the solidarity of sinners and righteous men.

Collective responsibility is a principle deeply rooted in the social order and religion of Israel. The Benjaminites all had to expiate the crime of the single town of Gibeah. And Sodom, from the youngest to the oldest men, was wholly responsible for sin. But Abraham tried to apply the same principle in reverse. If there is solidarity, and all must share the same destiny, why could not the righteous men save the sinners? Why make the righteous perish with the sinners, but not save the latter with the former?

Abraham figured that there were fifty righteous men. But if there were not that many, he continued praying, finally reducing the number to ten. He did not come down to one person, because less than ten would not comprise a collectivity. The individual alone did not count.

The prophets of Israel later became fully aware of the consequences of this principle, and attempted to correct it. The individual became separable from the community and responsible for himself alone.

The fathers shall not be put to death for their children, nor shall the children be put to death for the fathers; every man shall be put to death for his own sin.[21]

In those days they shall no longer say: "The fathers have eaten sour grapes, and the children's teeth are set on edge." But every one shall die for his own sin; each man who eats sour grapes, his teeth shall be set on edge.[22]

Son of man, when a land sins against me by acting faithlessly, and

[20] Gen. 4:10.   [21] Deut. 24:16.
[22] Jer. 31:29–30;see Ezek. 18:2.

I stretch out my hand against it, and break its staff of bread and send famine upon it, and cut off from it man and beast, even if these three men, Noah, Daniel and Job, were in it, they would deliver but their own lives by their righteousness.[23]

However, solidarity or someone's intercession have known more generous means and happier successes than are found in the story of Abraham. Not only ten righteous men, but even the intercession of a single one, was effective in saving a whole people in other circumstances.

But Moses besought the Lord his God, and said, "O Lord, why does thy wrath burn hot against thy people, whom thou hast brought forth out of the land of Egypt with great power and a mighty hand?"[24]

> *Therefore he said he would destroy them—*
> *had not Moses, his chosen one,*
> *stood in the breach before him,*
> *to turn away his wrath from destroying them.[25]*
> *Run to and fro through the streets of Jerusalem,*
> *look and take note!*
> *Search her squares to see*
> *if you can find a man,*
> *one who does justice*
> *and seeks truth;*
> *that I may pardon her.[26]*

And I sought for a man among them who should build up the wall and stand in the breach before me for the land, that I should not destroy it; but I found none.[27]

The Servant of the Lord took upon himself the punishment intended for the many, and by himself alone the many were saved.

> *Surely he has borne our griefs*
> *and carried our sorrows;*
> *yet we esteemed him stricken,*
> *smitten by God, and afflicted.*

[23] Ezek. 14:13s.
[24] Ex. 32:11.
[25] Ps. 106:23.
[26] Jer. 5:1.
[27] Ezek. 22:30.

But he was wounded for our transgressions,
he was bruised for our iniquities;
upon him was the chastisement that made us whole,
and with his stripes we are healed.[28]

But Abraham did not continue his bargaining down to one person. Lot, the righteous man, would have been enough. Or would not Abraham himself, and his prayer, have been sufficient? Did he not enter into solidarity with Sodom by his intercession?

The tragedy of this story is that in such circumstances Abraham was unable to save Sodom. Neither hospitable Lot nor any righteous men who may have been in the city could save it. In fact, nobody could save it. When Yahweh desires to save, He seeks someone Himself, who will enter the breach, or who intercedes, or who takes the sins of others upon himself. Or Yahweh saves by His own hand, even if there is not a single righteous man. But Yahweh had decreed the destruction of Sodom. What, then, was the purpose of Abraham's intercession?

In the story of Sodom, Abraham's prayer was not primarily a request to spare the lives of the guilty. He neither asked for pardon nor invoked mercy. Above all else, he was praying for the manifestation of Yahweh's *justice.*

In this instance, Yahweh was not the God who pardons or saves. He was not the Father or the Lord, patient and compassionate. Yahweh was the God who could exercise self-manifestation by destroying. He destroyed in order to show forth His justice.

Abraham invoked the "Judge of all the earth." And he said to Yahweh, "Far be it from thee to be unjust!" If there had been fifty righteous men in the city, Yahweh could have done them an injustice. If there had been ten, even then He would have been unjustly destroying. Abraham's bargaining simply served to make Yahweh's justice more apparent, thus preventing the manifestation from having any semblance of injustice. And Abraham continued down to the minimum number so that Yahweh's justice

[28] Is. 53:4–5.

would appear at its maximum. In reality, there was only one righteous man, and he saved himself. In him Yahweh's justice was saved to the fullest extent. And this, tragically, was all that mattered in the story.

It is true that the appeal to justice could have been a motive of persuasion, like a threat, or an accusation of injustice. And perhaps the prayer, out of context, could have had this sense. But in the context of the story it is justice that matters first and most. Abraham's prayer was like a precaution: "Let it not be said that in destroying the city you will be destroying some righteous man, for soon men could no longer be able to speak of your justice."

The story reveals Yahweh's justice and Abraham's justice as well.

[The Lord said,] ". . . for I have chosen him, that he may charge his children and his household after him to keep the way of the Lord by doing righteousness and justice; . . ."[29]

By demanding Yahweh's justice, Abraham showed his own exigency of justice. The people who would follow him would learn how he was righteous and how every son of Abraham must be righteous also.

The story also makes mention of Lot's justice. "This fellow came to sojourn, and he would play the judge!"[30] The story lays stress upon his justice against the background of Sodom's injustice. It was this injustice that made of him a judge, by his presence alone. A resident alien, like the Levite of Ephraim in Gibeah, was the only just man in Sodom. All the others were unjust.

But why this manifestation of the justice of Yahweh, Abraham, and Lot, at the cost of Sodom's life?

Abraham and Lot were both immigrant foreigners in the country. And both were righteous men. Indeed, they were the only just men in the country, or the story makes them appear so. Yahweh was also an immigrant, who had arrived with Abraham. And He is a just God, the only God who requires justice, and who is "the Judge of all the earth."

[29] Gen. 18:19.   [30] Gen. 19:9.

By contrast, the inhabitants of the country were all sinners, "from the youngest to the oldest." But the country could not endure such sin in its midst. "And the land became defiled, so that I punished its iniquity, and the land vomited out its inhabitants."[31]

Abraham was destined to be the father of a great nation, and also the symbol of justice. The land itself was awaiting this great nation, for the peoples who occupied it had become intolerable. When their evil was full to the brim, Yahweh delivered them over into the hands of this nation. By means of this story it can be seen that the newly arrived strangers were the only ones who could occupy the country by right of justice. Sodom was a little episode in this drama.

Lot had separated from Abraham, and he chose Sodom for his residence. On the edge of the country of the promises, there was a rich and covetable land. Lot had to abandon it, as Adam had abandoned the primitive paradise. Not by any fault of his own, like Adam, but rather like Noah, a righteous man, the only one who saved himself from the Flood.

Lot made another choice, and this time he chose Zoar. But soon after, he "went up out of Zoar, and dwelt in the hills with his two daughters, for he was afraid to dwell in Zoar."[32] In reality, it was because Lot still did not feel at home in the city, for he was a nomad of the hill-country. Neither Sodom nor Zoar was the right place for him. Away from the city, his daughters made him the father of two peoples who later established themselves on the borders of the Promised Land.

The story prepares in Lot the origin of Ammon and Moab, and by separating Lot from Abraham it separates the latter nations from the land of the patriarch. Abraham remains with his descendants and his God as the only rightful possessors of the Promised Land.

When Abraham reached the high lookout and saw that smoke covered the cities, he could only conclude that full justice had been done. Justice had been done both to Lot and to the inhabi-

[31] Lev. 18:25.   [32] Gen. 19:30.

tants of Sodom. God had manifested His justice, and Abraham's prayer had been the prayer of a just man, to which Yahweh had also done justice. However—it could be said—such a price to pay for this new manifestation of justice!

It must seem that Abraham's prayer for Sodom was a most dreadful prayer. And perhaps it would be better not to call it prayer at all, for prayer is more merciful. Its subject matter was wholly pragmatic, as an attempt to portray a terrible lesson that cost four cities.

When seen from the perspective of Sodom, it is a horrible story. But in the pedagogical plan of biblical history it is merely a small episode which, without consideration for Sodom, presents in a pictorial manner a demonstration of private providence. Unquestionably, the historiographer regarded it from this point of view.

If the story's individual elements are considered one by one, it must be concluded that Sodom, Abraham, and even Yahweh Himself are all equally symbols. All are stylized elements conserving nothing more than the figure of their real being. The pedagogical purpose modifies them and deprives them of normal verisimilitude in order to make them mere signs of figurative language.

In a world of ordinary reality there could not be a Sodom without any goodness, with no beauty whatever, and without ten righteous men. Nor is Abraham possible as a man of absolute rectitude, who prays for mercy in the name of justice. Nor does Yahweh manifest Himself in human history as a God with no other aspects than justice. Otherwise, who could exist in His presence?

In this context of the pre-history of the people, the episode of Sodom presents a great thesis: Only the just will possess the land, or only those who actually receive the promise of the country are worthy to obtain its possession.

Tradition has constantly evoked this episode, because it possesses still other facets as pertinent in regard to Sodom as in any circumstances.

And Babylon, the glory of kingdoms, the splendor and pride of the Chaldeans, will be like Sodom and Gomorrah when God overthrew them.[33]

Edom shall become a horror; everyone who passes by it will be horrified and will hiss because of all its disasters. As when Sodom and Gomorrah and their neighbor cities were overthrown, says the Lord, no man shall dwell there, no man shall sojourn in her.[34]

On the day when Lot went out from Sodom fire and brimstone rained from heaven and destroyed them all—so will it be on the day when the Son of man is revealed.[35]

She [Wisdom] saved the just man from among the wicked who were being destroyed, when he fled as fire descended upon Pentapolis [the five cities].[36]

> *If the Lord of hosts*
> *had not left us a few survivors,*
> *we should have been like Sodom,*
> *and become like Gomorrah.*[37]

> *I overthrew some of you,*
> *as when God overthrew Sodom and Gomorrah,*
> *and you were as a brand plucked*
> *out of the burning;*
> *yet you did not return to me.*[38]

Truly, I say to you, it shall be more tolerable on the day of judgment for the land of Sodom and Gomorrah than for that town.[39]

And you, Capernaum, will you be exalted to heaven? You shall be brought down to Hades. For if the mighty works done in you had been done in Sodom, it would have remained until this day.[40]

[33] Is. 13:19.
[35] Lk. 17:29.
[37] Is. 1:9.
[39] Mt. 10:15.
[34] Jer. 49:17–18; see 50:40.
[36] Wisd. 10:6.
[38] Amos 4:11.
[40] Mt. 11:23.

101

Sodom was a lesson learned profoundly. Tradition has applied it extensively. And as He dealt with Sodom, Yahweh also treated His enemies, the enemies of His people. He saved those who were His own, those whom He wished to save, even as He saved the just men of Sodom. The chosen sons, rebellious and culpable, would have been like the sons of Sodom if Yahweh had not held them in His hand. But Yahweh could be merciful, even when His people were like the men of Sodom. And Sodom had long been a traditional symbol when the historiographer wrote the episode for the first time.

Apart from the symbolical character and pedagogical purpose of the story, Abraham could have been a real man, who actually prayed for an existing Sodom. If we admitted hypothetically that the story possesses this kind of historical reality, and that Abraham really interceded for the liberation of the cities, then his prayer would have various psychological and theological implications.

When the patriarch reached the high place in the early morning and discovered that his prayer had not been accepted, and if he felt nothing, the son of Abraham—the believer—arrives with him at the same place and feels a deadly shiver of fear. But there is no difference between the patriarch and the son who would now ask for clemency for Sodom. Either its real existence becomes evident in the story, or the story becomes alive again. At all times there is some just man praying for a threatened city. And at all times there is a city that needs an angel or a prophet.

Lifting up his hands to Yahweh, interceding for Sodom, Abraham is a figure as truly alive and present as though he were praying this very day and would have to repeat his prayer tomorrow. And surely we will find all the other elements of the story—God, Sodom, and the fire of destruction—also present on the stage of the world in our time. Whenever a son of Abraham lifts up his hands or prostrates himself in God's presence, asking for clemency for the world, he is making the same story a present reality.

102

That is why it is tragic to arrive with Abraham at the same place of lookout, only to discover smoke over the cities. We would wish that Abraham had remained in Yahweh's presence, continuing to bargain with Him, until he had finally ascertained that not a single righteous man was still in the city. We wish that he had then resorted to other means of salvation. Is that not what is really done when someone tries to save something which is threatened?

Abraham, or a son of Abraham, ought to continue praying to Yahweh, and not withdraw to his tent. The dialogue must not be interrupted. The "I" must not allow the "Thou" to terminate the encounter until an answer has been obtained, a granting of grace, which does not depend on human merit. What guarantee based on such a weak condition could ever be secure?

The angels of destruction have not ceased to come down from above and to move through the world. Like the angels of Sodom, men also move through the world passing judgment. Is it not man himself who declares a city to be horrible and proclaims it anathema?

Perhaps it was because of some scandal that the demon of judging entered into man. Was he scandalized by seeing God's judgment? Or by seeing how the human imagination pictures God as a Judge?

Nevertheless, God must know His world, its firmness and its weakness. As its creator, He knows it well. The potter knows his vessel, and he knows the material used in making it, and where cracks or fissures are likely to appear. God must surely know man whom He created. He made man as he is. And He knows what to expect of him, since it is God Himself who determined the limits of man's strength.

> As a father pities his children,
>   so the Lord pities those who fear him.
> For he knows our frame;
>   he remembers that we are dust.[41]

41 Ps. 103:13–14.

If thou, O Lord, shouldst mark iniquities,
Lord, who could stand?
But there is forgiveness with thee,
that thou mayest be feared.[42]

If, therefore, God Himself destroys one of His own works as something badly done, is it not God who incites insolent criticism? How can man abstain from being critical, if the Creator Himself declares His work to be badly accomplished? However, when is it God who is exercising judgment, and when is it really man who attributes to God the judgment passed upon his own works?

Man learned to distinguish between good and evil, and arrogated to himself the faculty of passing judgment. Dressed as a judge, man could expel Adam from paradise, as Yahweh did. He could destroy mankind with the flood, saving only one man. He could destroy Sodom and liberate Lot. He could excommunicate a whole people from the human community and admit another that esteems his law. Man learned to distinguish between good and evil, and made himself a judge.

But when man believes himself capable of distinguishing things so perfectly, has he really done full justice? Is anything wholly evil even possible? Is there anything completely good?

Existence and perfection are incompatible qualities in the real world that we know. The existent is relative and perfection is absolute. Existence and imperfection are the clay of which all creatures in this world are made. Without this familiar contrast of existence and imperfection, the world would be inconceivable. It would be something else which it is not given to us poor creatures of this existent world to know. Absolute perfection is a utopia which the world is forever seeking, without ever finding it, and perhaps not even moving nearer to it.

If you want to possess the world, there can be no justice, and if it be justice that you want, you cannot have the world. You cling to both

[42] Ps. 130:3–4.

extremes: you want both the world and justice. But if you do not yield a little, the world cannot subsist.[43]

There is no city in the world that is divine. Nor is any city satanic. There is no nation that is just, nor any that is unjust. No man is full of light, nor is there any man full of darkness. If anyone sets himself up as a standard of justice, he would rightly provoke the indignation of everyone else.

If good and evil, beauty and ugliness, are always found in pairs within everyone, how can Lot's separation from Sodom's midst be justified? If Lot really belonged to the city, the latter would have lost its own being without him. Was it really Yahweh who separated him, or was it human judgment?

Lot saved himself from Sodom and became the father of the Moabites and Ammonites, two nations that were enemies of the people of Yahweh. Abraham was father of the Chosen People, who were to practice justice and rectitude. But were they not the same people among whom Yahweh would search in vain for a single righteous man in order to extend mercy through him to the others?

Abraham looked up to Yahweh and invoked the solidarity of righteous men in favor of the wicked. But there were not ten just men in the city. Certainly, there could not have been any one man who was wholly righteous. But in the midst of Sodom there was necessarily more goodness than could be found in ten men, sown in this field of corruption.

Add up the [good] actions of all [the inhabitants of Sodom], and the result will be fifty. . . . Add yourself to them, and they will amount to fifty.[44]

Add up Abraham's prayer, and the goodness and beauty of children and men and animals, the plants that perish, and of all nature, and you will have the number sufficient for salvation, or your justice will not be evident, if you condemn.

[43] *Bere'sit Rabbâh,* 49:9.   [44] *Bere'sit Rabbâh,* 49:9.

105

[The Lord said to Jonah,] "You pity the plant, for which you did not labor, nor did you make it grow, which came into being in a night, and perished in a night. And should not I pity Nineveh, that great city, in which there are more than a hundred and twenty thousand persons who do not know their right hand from their left, and also much cattle?"[45]

If Abraham were to pray for Sodom again, he would not leave the presence of Yahweh. He would not let the terrible Numinous enter into direct contact with things. It was for this reason that he was a prophet—to transform the bivalent Numinous from a power of destruction into beneficence; and to speak in God's name, like Moses, and not let the people perish.

If Abraham were to pray for Sodom again, he would not let the angels of destruction take Lot away with them. Lot and the inhabitants of Sodom were together. All alike belonged to the city. There could be no Sodom without Lot, and Lot outside of Sodom instantly loses the whole purpose of his existence. Why should the parts of a whole be separated? The angels destroyed Sodom in the same act whereby they brought Lot out of it, before spreading the fire.

What advantage was there in setting apart one man, and what was the reason for it? One day it was Noah who was set apart from the world, and on another occasion it was Lot who was liberated from Sodom, and finally a single people was given preference over all other nations. Does it mean that the one that is set apart will be different? Is God a respecter of persons, or who, if not He, does the setting apart?

The least unjust cannot be set apart. If anyone separates them, as if they were to set themselves apart, what would their function be? For what reason are they the best men in the midst of the wicked, if not to maintain the balance and neutralize the power of evil?

If Abraham were to pray for Sodom again, he would not let Yahweh go away. Nor would he invoke Yahweh's justice. Justice

[45] Jon. 4:10–11.

is a great goodness in human nature, and that is why man imagines it as an attribute of God. But justice is not the only good, nor can it be found in everything. Pure justice only exists as a mere rationalization. Nor does God possess justice as His only attribute, for He could not then possess the synthesis of goodness.

In a spontaneous prayer, Abraham would not have invoked justice alone. To entreat the "Judge of all the earth" to do justice is the same as imploring Him to destroy. If theological speculation is content to make justice the fundamental prerogative of Yahweh, then there can only be abjectness before Him, a universal confession of our own justice. But it can never be fitting to ask for mercy and grace in the name of human justice.

Spontaneous prayer, ever since man first began to pray, has invoked God in terms of a father benefactor, mighty to pardon and protect. It hopes and believes that God can be moved by the supplicatory voice of the humble, and let His wrath be changed into compassion. Spontaneous prayer finds in God a place for mercy.

Mercy is another kind of goodness in human relations. For that reason it is also considered an attribute of God. But if justice is primary, how can the two be combined? Mercy is a frank diminution of justice, a diminution or abrogation as a sign of goodness. Justice must yield to mercy in order that the latter may co-exist, and the former be entirely a good. At least this is how it appears when seen with reference to man. And if this analogy in no way enables us to speak of the divine, how is it possible to speak of God at all?

The most perfect prayer would say, "Thy will be done." But with Sodom threatened, the mediator hearing about it could only resort to intercession. The prayer that intercedes for others cannot be like philosophical resignation or contemplation. The one who prays is speaking with God in human language. He hopes his prayer can somehow enter into God's designs and affect them in the way that the human heart allows itself to be affected.

But in the story of Sodom there is no place for mercy. Justice rescued Lot from the catastrophe, but did not save anyone else. Mercy did not exist, and that is why everything perished except Lot. It was not Yahweh who destroyed Sodom, but His justice alone, fictitiously separated from Himself.

The prayer for Sodom was a tragic experience. How could Abraham, thereafter, ask anything of Yahweh? He does whatever He finds to be just, by Himself alone. Yahweh saved Lot, although Abraham had not asked that it be done; otherwise His justice would perish.

Yahweh marked out the way. Could Abraham have done better? But Abraham ought to have invoked Yahweh by some other name, not as the Judge, but as the Father. He should have asked for mercy rather than justice. When a man asks a favor, he is not in a position to demand justice. In the name of mercy, Yahweh would not have set Lot apart, nor turned a deaf ear to Abraham's request. Above all, He would have added Himself, Yahweh, to the side of favor.

Is man great or small among other creatures? Does he have more significance before Yahweh than they? If he is more significant, what is the world without men? And what is Sodom, completely destroyed? The Psalmist would have said, "Can the dead glorify thee, or can those who sleep in Sheol sing unto thee?" If Yahweh had been merciful to Sodom, it would have lived on to sing its everlasting gratitude. Beneath the ruins it proclaims justice, but the song of Sodom is the song of the dead.

If Abraham were to pray for Sodom again, he would not appeal to the rights of just men. There were just men in Sodom. There are just men in the world, some of them very great, like Abraham and Lot. But who can say whether human righteousness would be sufficient to demand any rights! It would be better, instead, to invoke Yahweh's mercy in behalf of just men, and their solidarity with the others.

108

THE JOURNEY
TO MORIAH

*When I first read this story I felt an im-
mense compassion for little Isaac.*
*Later, I understood that it was not the son,
but old Abraham, who was the hero of the
story.*
*Now when I read it again I see the destinies
of all believers profoundly engaged in the
journey to Moriah.*

So Abraham rose early in the morning, saddled his ass; and took two
of his young men with him, and his son Isaac: and he cut the wood
for the burnt offering, and arose and went to the place of which God
had told him.[1]

As though it was a festival day, his eyes opened widely, no
longer heavy with sleep. His body was agile, as when a man sets
out to accomplish something important. He drew aside the cur-
tain of heavy skins that covered the door-way of his tent, raised
his eyes and looked out upon the empty plains.

If he had noticed it, he would have seen the first herald of the
dawn on one of the four horizons, lighting the sands of the
colorless desert.

But he did not allow himself this gesture. There was no need
to rest his eyes upon anything, in order to give himself a few
moments of reflection.

[1] Gen. 22:3.

Everything had been decided, and the entire day was far too short to make the journey.

Rising early in the morning, Abraham hurriedly made his preparations. Quite methodically, he prepared all the things that were necessary, and only them, with no indecision, like someone who does the same thing every day of his life, or who had been awaiting this day for many years.

Abraham rose early in the morning, and without waking Sarah or the servants he took what he needed and set out upon the journey. The little band walked with rigorous steps over the ridges of the desert. Only the biting of their sandals in the sand could be heard.

On the horizon, in the direction towards which Abraham was heading, the sky took on the red color that is usual at dawn, but this time it suggested the image of a fire of holocaust upon a holy hill. And then Abraham, while continuing to walk, remembered one by one the words which had wakened him in the night.

"Take your son, your only son Isaac, whom you love, and go to the land of Moriah, and offer him there as a burnt offering upon one of the mountains of which I shall tell you."[2]

As though only one were not enough, there are four successive terms, each of them more specific, removing all possibility of equivocation: *your son, your only son—Isaac—whom you love.* The four terms could only mean one thing.

An observer would synthesize the narrative in the equation of Isaac—Moriah. He would consider all the rest as superfluous.

But Abraham perfectly understood the reason for the four terms. Each of them was a sonorous pulsation deep within his sensibility. Together they formed a litany of tenderness, with a painful background of tragedy.

Abraham understood all of its significance. The terms were spoken with a father's heart. And the observer's equation is inaccurate. The equation is properly Abraham—Moriah.

[2] Gen. 22:2.

110

Isaac was still far from Moriah. A long journey separated him from it, a journey which only Abraham's heart had already made. From the beginning the victim was his son, his only son, the one whom he loved, whom he loved in his heart. Abraham had already reached Moriah by anticipation.

Abraham indeed had a son, an only son. (The son of the slave woman has no part in the story.)

Abraham had special reasons for loving this son. In him, Abraham loved the future. for which he had renounced his entire past.

One day Abraham had given up his home, his kinsmen and his native land in order to become the father of a great people.[3]

Another day, he had witnessed the birth of a son in his tent. This was a son impossible to nature, a son of grace. "Now Abraham and Sarah were old, advanced in age, it had ceased to be with Sarah after the manner of women."[4] But Abraham had received a son by grace, because he had believed in him, although impossible, having previously renounced all that was possible.

And now a voice said to him, "*Take your son, your only son Isaac, whom you love, . . .*" In other words, take the past which you renounced, the present which you possess by grace, and the one who gives you the future you have awaited, and journey forth towards the land of Moriah.

Abraham rose early in the morning, and set out upon the journey towards the place which God had indicated to him.

On the third day Abraham lifted up his eyes and saw the place afar off.[5]

It had been a long journey of three endless days. Three days without succession or passing hours, without reference to anything whatever. It was a period in Abraham's life that began when he started out upon the journey and was interrupted when he lifted up his eyes and saw the place from afar.

[3] Gen. 12:1–2.   [4] Gen. 18:11.
[5] Gen. 22:4.

111

Abraham had lost sight of the tent in which a son had been born to him. He lowered his eyes, and followed a trail. And when he looked up, he was within sight of Moriah.

There was much time for reflection. The trail was difficult, because one could lose one's way. But Abraham did not alter his direction or retrace his steps. He did not change his mind, or put himself in disagreement. He neither suspended his assent nor refused to make the offering.

Abraham walked and walked and walked, and when he was already in sight of it from afar, he lifted up his eyes and saw Moriah.

Then Abraham said to his young men, "Stay here with the ass; I and the lad will go yonder and worship, and come again to you."[6]

On the horizon, within sight, was Moriah. Abraham and the boy had to go there. And "there" was the end of the journey.

The mount was a goal without return. Abraham could hardly have spoken of *coming back*. What unlikely hope could there have been in those words? Were they really words of hope, or simply a formula of peace for the others, in contrast with his own desperate resignation?

With Moriah in view, Abraham took leave of his little retinue. From all of them. He had been summoned to Moriah and he had to arrive there. It was entirely his own obligation, and terribly personal.

There at his side was his little son. But was Isaac really there, or was he absent and quite ignorant of all that Abraham's journey implied?

And Abraham took the wood of the burnt offering, and laid it on Isaac his son; and he took in his hand the fire and the knife. So they went both of them together.[7]

Abraham took the fire and the knife in his hand. And he went. Isaac, with the wood, also went along.

[6] Gen. 22:5.   [7] Gen. 22:6.

They went together. But the knife did not cut into the boyish body, nor could the fire burn the wood that Isaac was carrying on his shoulders. There was only a discreet distance between them, the same that separated Isaac's body from Abraham's.

The fire and the knife were with Abraham. And the patriarch felt in his flesh the cold of the iron and the voracity of the fire. The wood on Isaac's shoulders was not burning.

And they both walked together. each remote from the other. At the end, however, between these two estranged worlds there developed a lamentable nearness.

And Isaac said to his father Abraham, "My father!" And he said, "Here am I, my son." He said, "Behold, the fire and the wood; but where is the lamb for a burnt offering?" Abraham said, "God will provide . . . , my son." So they went both of them together.[8]

Until then, the grey desert had kept all feelings impenetrable. The trail was elusive, like a rigid line in a depopulated world. The one accompanied the other imaginatively, but only felt that he was traveling alone. They were traveling together, but they also walked alone. Each of them was alone.

And inasmuch as they were traveling alone, the familiar sound of their steps was like a dialogue concerning the ties that united them. The human aspects of this discourse affected them, and finally they both spoke aloud: "My father!" . . . "My son!" Pronounced in that moment, the two terms seem to have still kept their full meaning. For Isaac, at least, this was so. But what meaning did these terribly human expressions have for Abraham?

Abraham had relinquished Isaac when he left his tent. But he was the only one who knew this, and he kept the secret for himself. Nevertheless, when he said "my son," it seems as though there was in his words a primary paternal instinct to save, to preserve for himself, and to retain. Was there not still time to refuse to offer up his son on Moriah?

Isaac asked a question, being human and quite unaware of

[8] Gen. 22:7–8.

Abraham's tragedy. But in that moment his questioning was heavily ponderous. Nor could anyone with a more sinister sign have asked questions at such a moment.

Abraham could not answer Isaac's question. His reply was merely an evasion, hinting at mystery. "God will provide . . . , my son." And while he was saying "my son," he was flaming the fire and holding the knife in his hand.

Moriah was in sight. Only there could Abraham reveal the agreement between himself and God. Or let God reveal it. Abraham could not understand it, but he had entered into the agreement. It was best to let God reveal it.

And "God will provide" on Moriah. That is what Moriah means.[9]

Abraham could have made a brutal confession, understandable to everyone, according to his own understanding. But Abraham had long before given up trying to understand. What he did understand was simply an absurdity of deadly seriousness. And before accepting this implacable absurdity and sharing it with others, he had decided to make no attempt to understand. He did not know whether he could recover his son or not. But the God who had spoken to him, against all hope, still made him hopeful.

Abraham declined to give an answer to his son. He left it to

[9] The name Moriah (*Moriyyah*) in this tory is the name of a country. The place where it is supposed that Yahweh commanded Abraham to go is a particular location within this country, but its name is not mentioned. From the time of Chronicles (II Chron. 3:1), if not before, the name *Moriah* was expressly applied to the mountain of the Temple of Jerusalem, and this was continued in subsequent tradition. In the present story, the name lends itself to a theological interpretation, because of its popular etymology. According to this etymology, it is a name composed of *rââh* (to see) and *Yah* (Yahweh), meaning "Yahweh will see" or "Yahweh will provide." But in the same story, perhaps because the actual Masoretic punctuation must be retained, there is another version of the name: on the mountain "Yahweh will let Himself be seen" or "Yahweh will show Himself." This interpretation of the name is an allusion to the apparition of the angel at the story's end. Perhaps the present story synthesizes two different traditions, each based upon a particular interpretation of the name Moriah. Morphologically, the name *Moriyyah* does not coincide with either of the two interpretations. Both have interpreted it *ad sensum,* and give it a role in the theological content of the story.

114

the wisdom of the God who could provide. Isaac, in any case, could not have understood the absurdity of his brutal confession.

Consequently, Abraham's reply left them both as estranged as before. It was merely a lost opportunity for drawing nearer together.

The two of them walked on together, yet each was alone. Drawing the boy into Abraham's mystery would have made him a suffering victim too, by putting him on Moriah ahead of time.

When they came to the place of which God had told him, Abraham built an altar there, and laid the wood in order, and bound Isaac his son, and laid him on the altar, upon the wood. Then Abraham put forth his hand, and took the knife to slay his son.[10]

Following their arrival on Moriah, the author did not omit a single gesture of Abraham's hand. Observing Abraham, one would see him dispose of everything in an orderly way, without faltering or anxiety, even lifting the knife without trembling.

On the other hand, the author says absolutely nothing about Isaac at this moment. Should he have done differently? In reality, the author was not telling about Isaac in this story. He refers to "the son," that is, to Abraham's paternity. That is why Isaac's role was silent.

If he had mentioned more about Isaac, it would be the story of a crime. Or a description of a human sacrifice.[11] But it is

[10] Gen. 22:9–10. In Jewish tradition, this story is not called "the sacrifice of Isaac" but "the binding of Isaac" ('agedat Yitzhak). In fact, the external action of Abraham ended in the binding, and did not go as far as the sacrifice.

[11] Some commentators think that the pedagogical purpose of this story is the abolition of the practice of human sacrifices, known in Canaan (see Lev. 20:2–5; Deut. 12:31; 18:10) and practiced until a late period by the Israelites (see II Kings 16:3; 21:6; 23:10; Jer. 7:31; 19:5–6; 32:35 Ezek. 16:21). The first-fruits of men, animals, and harvests belonged properly to Yahweh. But the first-born sons of men, according to the Law, had to be substituted or ransomed (Ex. 13:11 ff.; Lev. 17:21; Num. 18:15). It does not seem, however, that this is the purpose of the story, at least in its present state. Its real meaning is found in the "testing" of Abraham's fidelity. This is confirmed by the promises repeated after his triumph. The theme of human sacrifices could have been primary in some other narration of the story, but this is not so in the story as we know it.

neither the one nor the other, because it is not the story of Isaac.

Isaac was really absent. As far as Abraham was concerned, Isaac was already lost to him, several days before. Abraham lost Isaac by renunciation, when he rose early one morning and began the journey. All the rest is the story of Abraham.

Abraham extended his hand, grasped and raised the knife, not in order to lose Isaac, but rather *to perform a rite.*

God could have taken little Isaac by His own hand, and Abraham would then have been deprived of him. Or Abraham could have lifted up the knife in his tent, where he had made the renunciation of his son. And yet he went with Isaac to Moriah. He went there to perform a pedagogical rite.

Abraham was not an assassin, nor the hero of a tragedy. He was the executor of a rite.[12] Abraham went to Moriah, but he had already done the deed in his tent. He had not raised the knife there, but he had made the renunciation of Isaac.

The rite which Abraham performed was carried out when he climbed Moriah in order to "worship" and then returned, as he had told his servants. To climb Moriah so that God would provide, as he had said to Isaac.

But how would God provide, while the knife was raised in Abraham's hand before the frightened eyes of Isaac?

But the angel of the Lord called to him from heaven, and said, "Abraham, Abraham!" And he said, "Here am I." He said, "Do not lay your hand on the lad or do anything to him; for now I know that you fear God, seeing you have not withheld your son, your only son, from me."[13]

[12] That is why I believe it is out of place to raise an ethical problem here, or to define the act as "a theological suspension of morality," as Kierkegaard would say. This aspect is completely absent from the historiographer's mind. The present story has a pragmatic finality. All of the themes are subordinate to one, and all of the elements serve the central theme. Consequently, diverting attention to secondary problems and elements is to disregard the historiographer's purpose and introduce motives which do not exist in the story.

[13] Gen. 22:11–12.

The story concludes with a triumphant apotheosis. High on Moriah, Isaac had just been born. Abraham recovered him forever.

God had not resurrected Isaac, but He had granted him life. Abraham had not engendered him again, but acquired him in a new dimension of paternity.

The Isaac born on Moriah was doubly the son of Abraham's faith. The father obtained him, not as the fruit of his aged flesh, but rather as the creation of his youthful faith.

Abraham finally understood the mystery of Moriah. He had seen God's way of "providing." He knew that God could make his son's dead body live, as He had made his own body live, and Sarah's also. He knew that in God's hand was the power to make him the father of a great people, even without Isaac. What he did not know was how. But now he saw that God not only had not deprived him of Isaac, but had even made Isaac more profoundly his son than before.

Abraham's deed facilitated the designs of God, inasmuch as it transformed his fatherhood. God had been seeking a people who could be better through faith. And Abraham engendered in Isaac a nation of people who were entirely sons of his faith. For just as the Isaac acquired on Moriah owed nothing to Abraham's flesh, but was wholly the son of the first and second impulsion of his faith, so likewise the people to be born of Isaac would be sons only of Abraham's faith.

Faith was not, therefore, a monster gradually devouring whatever the patriarch possessed. At the end, Abraham not only kept what he had, but acquired much more. He gained everything without losing his son. Far from losing Isaac, he acquired him as the son of his faith. And if it be hazardous to fatherhood to engender by the flesh, it is a much greater risk to engender a son by faith.

Abraham retraced his steps, triumphantly making the journey in four days. He returned after "worshipping" and after God had been able to "provide." A whole company of peoples traveled with him over the ridges of the desert. And Sarah awaited him at the door-way of the tent. Abraham held in his hand little Isaac and all of the nation that had just been born to him. They were a people who would invoke the name of the God of Abraham forever, and would remember Abraham as the "father of their faith."

The story continues with a second apparition of the angel who renews the promise to him.

"By myself I have sworn, says the Lord, because you have done this, and have not withheld your son, your only son, I will indeed bless you, and I will multiply your descendants as the stars of heaven and as the sand which is on the seashore. And your descendants shall possess the gate of their enemies, and by your descendants shall all the nations of the earth bless themselves, because you have obeyed my voice."[14]

This reading of the story, with comments, has been an attempt to approach the figure of Abraham psychologically, in this concrete episode of his tradition. However, far from claiming that this is the only way to approach him, or even the most conformable with the spirit of the story, it is merely one of many ways.

It is perhaps the most spontaneous way for anyone reading the story with simplicity of heart. If Abraham one day found himself in such a critical moment of peril as the historiographer describes, the only way to understand the situation is to enter into it oneself, filling up what is lacking in the description with whatever one would personally feel.

The entire force of the drama lies in the dilemma confronting the patriarch. Either he must obey the voice speaking to him and give up his son, or hold fast to Isaac, disobeying Yahweh's command. This is what constitutes the drama's plot, called a "testing."

However, what really produces astonishment is not the testing, but the serene and sure activities of the patriarch. If we try to understand them or attempt to follow the same rhythm and

[14] Gen. 22:15–18.

pattern, there is no point of support within reach. Reason does not follow his movements, and feeling rejects them.

In the perspective of reason, Abraham's action escapes all human logic. If we try to understand each of his steps, we encounter absurdity.

According to human logic, it was absurd for Abraham to rise early and set out for Moriah. Raising the knife was absurd and dreadful. And all of this in obedience to a mysterious voice commanding him to take Isaac's life, the son of his old age, the only one who could perpetuate his name in descendants.

The psychological approach cannot attain this summit. Either Abraham was a man in whom rational logic had no place, or he is a symbol at the outer margin of the human. If he was a bridge, connecting the extreme limits of rationality with another and different world, then the language of reason is not adequate to speak of his action.

Ever since we have known Abraham, from the time he left Ur of the Chaldeans, everything in him tended towards becoming the father of a numerous posterity. In the very moment when he could really hope for this, because God had given him a son, a voice in the night commanded him to relinquish him. It was the same voice that had granted him a son.

As soon as he abandoned his kinsfolk, while still capable of engendering, everything had been useless and absurd. In exchange for future hopes, he had given up everything that was real and tangible and present. He had renounced everything indeed, and had become a wanderer in foreign lands. All for the sake of his future. And now that he was raising his arm, what could he still expect from the future?

Would he return to his aged wife, only to see his name effaced in the dead silence of a tent lost in the desert?

However, even before reaching Moriah, Abraham had spoken of "worshipping" and "coming back," and of God who would "provide." What mysterious logic was hidden in Abraham's act?

119

Was there some other logic surpassing the logic which reason knows?

The story of Abraham's journey to Moriah begins with the words:

After these things God tested Abraham, and said to him, "Abraham!" And he said, "Here am I."[15]

In the pages of holy Scripture we often come upon "testings" of this kind. Often, the response of the person being tested is negative. But every positive response forever defines a "just" man.

When it is known from the beginning that this was a test of Abraham's fidelity, the reader is then free from the necessity of tragedy and irreparable horror. He waits entirely upon Abraham's response. And if Abraham wins out in the testing, it may not be clear how this was so, but somehow the reader will have avoided the horrible.

For Abraham, however, there was the deadly seriousness of a precise command, without the attenuation of a known testing that could lead to triumph. We make the whole journey with him and witness the spectacle of his greatness. But a tragedy remains possible, and there is the feeling of absurdity until the very end.

And since this was a testing and Abraham did not know it, what mysterious "logic" illumined Abraham's steps, enabling him to overcome what was obviously absurd?

Abraham cried out "Here am I!" in response to the voice that spoke to him in the night. This was not to indicate his location, but was an unconditional acceptance, a self-oblation. When the command is known, the response seems beyond understanding.

But the old patriarch had known this voice for a long time. He heard it the first time, and henceforth was always ready to hear it again. And it was completely irrational the first time also.

"Go from your country and your kindred and your father's house to the land that I will show you."[16]

[15] Gen. 22:1.   [16] Gen. 12:1.

And Abraham broke all ties with the past and the present, and set forth on his journey of hope. Necessarily, the voice which invited him to renounce everything, must have given him sufficient assurances. Reason does not know what these assurances were, but Abraham was able to believe.

By faith Abraham obeyed when he was called to go out to a place which he was to receive as an inheritance; and he went out, not knowing where he was to go.[17]

With this renunciation Abraham entered into a sphere of values in which the categories of reason have no entrance. In this sphere there must also be a form of logic. Abraham, of course, did not understand it; nevertheless, he accepted it and complied with all its demands.

Abraham saw the years passing. His vitality was diminishing, and still he had no descendant. In spite of this, however, by the pure force of his "logic," he went on counting descendants as numerous as the sands of the desert.[18]

One day Sarah placed little Isaac on Abraham's knees. This was the impossible son of his old age. "By faith Sarah herself received power to conceive, even when she was past the age, since she considered him faithful who had promised."[19]

However much Abraham felt himself to be a father, his happiness was not the kind familiar to normal fatherhood. Isaac was not the son of youthful vigor, which Abraham no longer possessed. Nevertheless, he was a father.

In his tent, with the joy that accompanies the birth of a child, Abraham began to possess a human and comprehensible thought and outlook. From that moment, he abandoned his irrational paradise, for now he had human motives for hope. Now at last his posterity had begun to germinate, which would be as numerous as the sands of the desert.

But with all this, Abraham had ceased to be. Abraham was

[17] Heb. 11:8.   [18] Gen. 15:5–6; 22:17.
[19] Heb. 11:11.

121

faith, and even without Isaac, he would have to believe in his posterity.

And one night God called Abraham again. And Abraham rose early in the morning to set out for Moriah.

He had made the renunciation of everything once again, the past, the present, and the rational future. He lifted up the knife over Isaac, the son of his faith and his flesh, and entered once more into the sphere of his "logic." It was not because of infinite resignation, but with the same hope which had been the sign of his life until now.

By faith Abraham, when he was tested, offered up Isaac, and he who had received the promises was ready to offer up his only son, of whom it was said, "Through Isaac shall your descendants be named." He considered that God was able to raise men even from the dead.[20]

If Abraham had not been willing to sacrifice his son, then his blind faith in leaving his native land would have been meaningless. And because of his advanced age, he could never have hoped to have a son of his own. By enduring the test of Moriah, Abraham remained what he was. He overcame Moriah and offered up the son who was partly the son of his flesh, in order to remain alone—with or without Isaac—with the son of his faith.

One by one, the acts and movements of Abraham, separated from the context of his entire life, are quite meaningless. They are all concatenated in a sphere that is not the sphere of reason's domain. Within their own sphere, each of his movements has its own "logic."

St. Paul, reckoning in this super-rational order of values, synthesized all of Abraham's characteristics in one single motive which, in theological tradition, has come to be considered as fundamental to the biblical figure of the patriarch.

In hope he believed against hope, that he [Abraham] should become the father of many nations; . . . He did not weaken in faith when he considered his own body, which was as good as dead. . . , or when he considered the barrenness of Sarah's womb.[21]

[20] Heb. 11:17–19.   [21] Rom. 4:18, 19.

According to St. Paul, the mystery of Abraham is simply the mystery of his faith, that is, his unconditional trust in the voice of God.

The heroism of all his illogical renunciation finds its application, if it is not a paradox, in the mystery of his faith.

It was faith that gave Abraham a son, both the first and the second time. It was faith that would give him as sons a whole multitude of peoples.

After all of these considerations, it is still difficult to suppose that we have really understood the figure of Abraham journeying toward Moriah. By the use of *rational* terminology, we have decided that his action was "logical," but only within the dialectic in which Abraham moved. But this dialectic and its logic, in attempting an explanation, finally took refuge in the mystery of faith. This gave us an "explanation" by means of a mystery!

The psychological or rational explanation of the patriarch's action is an audacious and empty pretension. In reality, it goes no further than mere phenomenology.

For anyone who adheres to the reasoning process alone, the whole drama takes place in a world of strange phenomena. Its language, like an unknown tongue, only speaks of the existence of an incomprehensible world.

But reading the story as a believer, the situation is different. The believer's approach is more knowing and certain, for he takes into account a whole world of values far beyond that of the rational world. The believer has within himself a point of reference and support that serves as an analogy to introduce him into the world of Abraham.

Nevertheless, Abraham's action appears as an extreme case, which the believer would ordinarily never encounter, even when obeying a super-rational dialectic. In real life such a crucial situation would be unimaginable, nor would it seem possible that such force could be found in any son of man.

If we think about the story again, perhaps it no longer conceals another version much less personal and human, in spite of its existential aspects. And this version has a thematic function.

The style and terminology of the story are not adequate to describe real and living persons, if it were not for the suggestion which its dramatic power exercises upon us, and the retrohistorical background of each character in the tradition. But a realistic existential picture with living persons could not be portrayed if it did not contain elements which are not found in the story.

We find in the story itself a prevalent serenity and rigid sureness of movement which would be improbable if it were the story of a real human person. Is Abraham a real person in this story?

In Pauline theology the figure of Abraham is summed up in a definition as simple as "father of faith." But even earlier, in ancient history, it was his function to be the witness of the God who had called him, simply by his trust in Him. His definition would then have been "the man who has trusted." This theme is superimposed to such an extent upon the personal characteristics of the patriarch that it seems to suppress them.

From the very beginning of his story we encounter a man superior to himself, so to speak. Abraham was greater than a real man. He was simply what Yahweh made of him. We know nothing about his physical likeness, and we are told nothing about his personal qualities. We only know about his vocation and mission.

From Ur to Moriah, Abraham served so perfectly as an instrument in Yahweh's hands that he seems like a message of divine action, rather than a mortal man moving by his own steps. The historiographer placed him on the road to Moriah like a statue, dead though traveling, that had no human feeling within itself.

Abraham is great, as a message and action of God are great. His story is the story of election. His figure becomes greater, the more it is simplified. In the greatest simplification, Abraham is reduced to the concept of *faith,* as John the Baptist is reduced to the concept of *voice.* But this single concept, free of the littleness of a real person, expresses all of the patriarch's greatness.

The story of Abraham, therefore, is not the story of a mortal being, but the story of a choice, and of one of God's designs. It is not the story of a man, but the idealized pre-history of the people of God.

Abraham, as a visual sign, was entirely at the service of this people. His vocation, his mission, his trust in Yahweh, his heroic deed on Moriah, everything—whether as real occurrences or merely as a visual sign—was for the sake of his posterity. Without the people to be born of him, the figure of Abraham disappears, and becomes meaningless and without purpose. His whole *raison d'être* was a social function.

It was his posterity that called Abraham out of his native land, and made him journey to all the places which his descendants would later inhabit. And this it was which gave him the object of his faith and hope, and made him what he was. His very name—Abraham—finally came to signify "father of a multitude," according to the interpretation of the people, so that absolutely everything would have reference to his descendants.[22]

The figure of Abraham consequently has a dimension far greater than that of a man. It has the greatness of a theological message.

The author who wrote about Abraham's action was thinking more of the divine purpose (the choice of a people in history), than of relating the ephemeral vicissitudes of a simple mortal man. The human basis to which he descends is the orchestration of his great theme within the framework of the story.

That is why Abraham is great and living, like the vitality and greatness of the theology which sustains the believer, Abraham's heir. And as a participant in the divine plan, Abraham's visible contribution was in witnessing for Yahweh, as an example of what it means to trust in Him. Abraham placed his intrumental-

[22] See our first chapter.

125

ity at Yahweh's disposal, and in himself, as in a symbol, the promises began to be fulfilled. Their terminal point was the choice of a people.

His descendants call him "Father Abraham." The whole history of Israel, in the theological vein in which it is written, could be formulated as the history of the vicissitudes of the promises made by Yahweh to Abraham in favor of his posterity.

And as the concept of Abraham grows larger as a symbol, so too the concepts of "people" and posterity increase progressively. St. Paul, without effort, felt able to include all peoples in the term "Abraham's posterity," once the universal *dynamics* of his person had surpassed ethnic limitations, thus attaining to a spiritual fatherhood without frontiers.

And as the son of Abraham's flesh was transformed into a son of his faith, so likewise the nation born of Isaac has been transformed into a spiritual community in which all peoples possess the right of citizenship. And the same Abraham who was father of the race is also father of the sons of faith, the father of all believers.

Abraham is a symbol. His journey to Moriah was not a personal drama, but the action of a model of fidelity. However, the elevation of Abraham to the status of a symbol and a model does not eliminate from his story a serious implication for his descendants. By depriving the story of personal limitations, it becomes more binding and obliging. It emerges from the private realm into a transcendental implication. As a symbol, it is the opening of the way in which the sons of Abraham must walk. What might have been the story of a man is instead a universal drama.

That is why the society that produced the story of Abraham did not consider it to be a splendid biography of a hero of the past, nor a pure work of art, commemorating the deed on Moriah. Abraham is a symbol, continuing to live in the present of his people and of all peoples who have shared in his inheritance.

All of his descendants are "sons of Abraham," not only those who are sons of the Law, but also the sons of the faith of Abraham, father of all believers.[23]

However, by transmitting this privileged status, the drama incarnate in Abraham is also transmitted. Accordingly, this is a serious implication, continually involving every believer. It means that the heir of the promises must enter into the dialectic of the patriarch's faith, which implies a willingness to rise early in the morning to take the road to Moriah, and to lift up the knife.

Abraham was primordial among believers, and the risk he took requires an equal willingness in his heirs. Abraham lives in his descendants, and the day when no believer is willing to repeat his action, his "logic" will have failed and all his posterity will have perished, together with the symbolical exemplification of the patriarch.

How can any mortal man repeat Abraham's action, taking the leap into the absurd and attaining finally to his "logic"?

If Abraham's journey to Moriah was not intended by the historiographer to be merely a personal and human drama, but a symbol of fidelity, neither can the bitter particular implications be required in applying the symbol to the believer. To apply the symbol in each of its details would not be in accordance with the historiographer's intention or the existential and human situation of the believer.

Abraham's action is an ideal and a model. It is a model and symbol of fidelity and trust. The action narrated in this story is not repeated every day, but it is a synthesis in which all of life is concentrated and in which the believer's whole attitude is formulated.

The psychological approach to the episode of Moriah can point out many other themes: tragedy, desperation, the suspension of ethics. But these themes do not easily accord with the spirit of the story.

In applying this symbolical story to the believer, the concept

23 Rom. 4:16.

of *faith* cannot be used in a strictly abstract manner. Through secular speculation this concept has acquired many shades of meaning which do not accord with the vital belief and trust of Abraham's story. But neither is the believer a pure abstraction of faith. Together with faith, there are other factors and other motives of action, called virtues and passions. Reality would not recognize a pure believer, because in fact he is a complex being, like any human being, impelled and importuned by many forces and counter-forces before each particular action.[24]

Nevertheless, if it is permissible to abstract a profound quality of the believer, election expresses itself, before all else, by faith. It is faith which brings the believer closest to Abraham's action. The history of the "sons of Abraham" is like a spectacle of pilgrims, with fire and knife in hand, resolute and audacious, on the road to Moriah.

Like the patriarch himself, anyone who puts faith into practice must be willing to give up whatever he possesses, whatever he sees and knows . . . for something he hopes to obtain. An act of faith is both credence and assent, a pursuit in quest of a voice that has spoken. An act of faith is renunciation of the Isaac born in the tent, for the Isaac to be born on Moriah.

But when the leap has been taken, the believer finds himself in the sphere of Abraham. In this sphere everything has its coherent "logic." Henceforth, Abraham's steps are understandable, and the believer can accompany him. The journey is meaningful, or is the only one with meaning and purpose. This is not a sense of resignation when there is a goal. The goal gives significance to every single step, whether taken towards acquisition or renunciation. There is neither resignation nor tragedy on the road to Moriah, but only hope and love.

[24] The terms in quotation marks reproduce expressions of Søren Kierkegaard (*Fear and Trembling*, New York, 1954). I believe, however, that his approach was not adequate to understand the figure of Abraham. Instead of seeing him as he appears in the pages of the Bible, he regarded him excessively from a psychological perspective, and even in this respect, under the unilateral prism of the pure believer.

What mysterious power was in the voice that called Abraham, transforming him and enabling him to overcome the weak condition of human nature? What vigor enabled him to reach journey's end and perform the superhuman act, in order soon to retrace his steps, triumphant?

ON THE MARGIN
OF HISTORY

The writer of history selects factual data of the human past and coordinates them, so as to draw out some meaning from them. On the margin of the chosen data, there are others, and with these there are unsuspected interpretations. That is why history is always being written anew.

The object of history is man himself. But the actions and passions of man are not completely substantiated in material that is suitable for the historian. For this reason, on the margin of the history that can be written, there still remains a great deal of man's history. And it is this which has greater probability of survival, because, although it is not written, it is transmitted alive in the depths of the human mind.

ACCORDING to the computation of the Bible, the space of time that stands between Abraham and ourselves is about four thousand years. Going back even two millenniums before Abraham, we would already be beyond the reach of history. This is not really a great distance, for interest in the past extends much further still. Where history ends, pre-history begins, and the latter has no determined frontiers. In this long stretch of time, Abraham was only of yesterday.

The motives which arouse modern man's interest in his past are many. And the value and quality of the methods used to reach it are many also. Some men possess a mere intellectual curiosity; others feel a sense of solidarity with whatever has existed before. And there are still others moved by a kind of urgent necessity to decipher and interpret the problems of man's origin.

This last motive was especially cherished by the generations that preceded us most closely. They attempted, perhaps somewhat arrogantly, to discover the human cradle, and to reveal, once and for all, the many mysteries concerning it.

It is unnecessary to remark that the attempt was not carried out without a certain humiliation, for the origin of the human species, like that of its beliefs, together with its practices and institutions, continues, as before, with veiled face, concealing its mysteries from science.

Another motive, more modest, for interest in the past, is the demand for light for the present. History is the "mistress of life" for anyone who desires it. Men of yesterday, in their time, had to confront problems similar to our own, seeking a solution to them. Their problems were many, certainly not less than the problems of today. They ranged from those that were physically peremptory, like the problem of their own subsistence, to the most clamorous demands of the spirit. These resembled the problems that now concern the sociologist, the statesman, the theologian, the economist.

According to the attitude and demands with which a person approaches the stage of history, he will find in it a whole range of different responses. The same remains of a civilization, discovered by the archeologist, prove to be of simultaneous importance for the anthropologist, the historian, the philologist, and the epigraphist, as for the economist and the collector of antiquities.

A cordial communion with the past brings it closer to the present. Patriotism identifies the man of today with the great

exploits of his nation. Religion identifies him with its soteriological history. The man who returns to the past by the roads of
patriotism or sympathy, religion or race, not only knows what
once existed, but enters within it with all of his human faculties,
constantly injecting new life into it. There is not a more
efficacious way to blot out space and time. Without any play on
words, and without metaphorical usage, it can certainly be said
that the past continues in the present.

However, in this case the way of approaching what once
existed is not the bare road of history. Together with history
there are other factors which only the philosopher or sociologist,
the psychoanalyst or the theologian would be able to define.
These factors largely escape the means and measures of pure
history, whose only sources of evidence are tangible materials
that can be empirically controlled and verified.

There are, consequently, apart from history, other ways to
enter into the domain of the past, or ways whereby the past can
make itself present. These are the ways followed by reasoning,
intuition, and feeling, in search of ultrasensible values and
realities empirically beyond control, which have been revealed
in the course of time.

Goethe believed that the writing of history is the best way
to free oneself of the burden of the past. Croce agreed with this
idea, and expressed it similarly. He said that the writing of history liberates us from history.

But this would not be the case when these other related factors
adopt the events of history as their vehicle and insist upon keeping the past operative in the present. It is not the historian's task
to transform the entire message of the past into a catalogue of
memories, or into mere material for thought. That which comes
affixed to related history, between the lines and on its margin,
is not subject to the historian's control. It is not found among
the elements of his narration.

In this pregnant perspective, the tradition or story of Abraham
must be given its proper place. Within it, Abraham is not only

of yesterday, but belongs to today also, and most certainly he belongs to tomorrow as well.

The person who follows Abraham's destiny along the much traveled roads, from his historical beginning among the Semitic peoples on the move, and in the history of Israel, in Judaism, in nascent Christianity, and in Islam, even down to the present day —all of them roads in which Abraham put his name—will recognize with surprise that the patriarch has a similar actuality in each of these spheres, as if he really belonged to each one.

How is this possible? How can a figure of obscure origin and incoherent history, whose very existence is often disputed, awaken the interest of widely separated eras, and of peoples of greatly different mentality and culture? Is it purely his historical personality that obtains this effect?

If it is carefully observed, the millenary figure of the patriarch is subject, in its multiform tradition, to continual transformations, each of which reveals in him some valid significance, which is not necessarily the same.

The Hebrew historian (and this is no more than a simplifica-tion, since all schools of thought have dealt with the story of Abraham), saw in the patriarch the common ancestor of the whole nation, the one who was chosen and blessed with promises which, by his personal fidelity, were fulfilled in his descendants. Late Judaism adorned his tradition with polychromatic anecdotes that made of his person a living example of religious virtues. Christianity, through St. Paul, held Abraham's faith in special esteem, and extending his fatherhood from the ethnic to the religious spheres, made him the father of all believers. This is the Abraham preferred by Christianity in the West, whereas the Eastern Church venerates him as a model of charity. Islam saw in the Hebrew patriarch the first champion of the purest mono-theism.[1]

One after the other, each new interpretation (perhaps with

[1] On the significance of Abraham in these traditions, see *Cahiers Sion-niens,* vol. 5, Paris, 1961.

the exception of the rabbinic) increasingly stripped the figure of Abraham of his personal characteristics, finally making him a pure symbol of abstract theological ideas. Accordingly, he was immunized against cultural anachronisms and liberated from the harsh contingencies which time and space impose upon every religious ordinance. Neither the primitive simplicity of the nomad, nor the ethnic particularism of the biblical version, nor its anthropomorphic crudeness, constitutes an obstacle to the persistent validity of any religious theme symbolized in the patriarch.

The effect is obviously due to the continual adaptation of the themes, and the ability of each generation to read between the lines or on the margin of history. The figure of Abraham is constantly actualized. In every situation and at every moment, the believer contemplates him beneath his own prism. For this very reason time is unable, for lack of actuality, to detain him in any of the stages of his story.

The repeated insistence upon actualization of the figure of the patriarch is neither accidental nor capricious. And it certainly cannot be attributed to the congeneric power of his nomadic personality. The insistence can be explained only with reference to the patriarch's universality and greatness, in the version of his figure given by the Yahwist author.

In addition to formulating themes of ethnic and national interest, valid for his immediate descendants, this ancient version makes of the patriarch a visual sign of universal values. Later versions merely defined and stylized these values, adapting them to their day and age. Consequently, a vigorous and conscious solidarity of successive generations with the same essential figure of the patriarch was maintained.

We have given consideration to some of these values in the preceding chapters, but they were only an indication of much more. However, instead of adding still other themes, a better simplification seems preferable. The figure of the patriarch serves as a sign of union, but even the themes themselves are all expressions of one central theme.

In abstract terms, the permanent message of Abraham can be reduced to this point: how God intervenes in human existence, and how this intervention, to express itself, encounters adequate symbols in history. (We are not concerned about the *factum* of divine intervention in the world, nor whether this belief, which is anthropologically universal, has a corresponding reality behind it. This could not be established on the basis of this story. It is only a question of *how* God intervenes.)

In the acceptance of the divine transcendence, and in this intervention of God in the world, two distinct terms, whose union is impossible, encounter each other. But how can God and man ever meet? How can there even be a relationship between God and history, the infinite and the finite, the Creator and creation, eternity and time?

Formulated in this way, with abstract terms, these concepts do not even remotely disturb the historiographer's attention. And perhaps that is precisely how he succeeded in stating a formula of encounter which no philosophy could improve upon.

Considered rationally, the encounter of God with the world of men is a drama without human proportions. Is it God who approaches man? Or is it man who approaches God and attains to Him? How can man endure such an experience unless a catastrophe occurs within him? Or does the catastrophe in fact take place in the encounter itself?

Today we would say that the encounter occurs on the frontiers or margin of reason's sphere. Why then did man discover *reason* and make it the measure of all realities? Within its limits there is no place for this encounter which is, nevertheless, a human experience, This means that *human* cannot be wholly equated with *rational*, not even as the measure of knowledge. Reason is only one aspect of man, or one of the ways which man possesses in making his approach to things. Complex reality extends far beyond the domain of reason. Or is the irrational unreal in man?

In that case, however, a great part of human experience would be unreal. And yet the experience of the numinous encounter is unquestionably a real experience.

Abraham is portrayed as someone who had this experience. But the conflict of the encounter did not perturb him. If there was any conflict, it was abated in the form of telling his story. There are no instances of faltering, nor any personal trivialities recorded. Every step proceeds with sureness until the quiet end.

The result is that Abraham obtains from the encounter a purpose for his life, and a clear and certain goal for all his descendants.

The conflict of the numinous encounter between God and Abraham seems to resolve itself, as a rational conflict, if it is remembered that in man there are other powers operating without reason's control. But the conflict appears to be stated in other terms when seen in the light of the story.

Successive interpretations of the figure of the patriarch all presuppose a historical Abraham at the base, although the personal and human story is not the center of attention. But if we turn to the critical historian of today, and ask him for the historical basis of the traditions of the patriarch, we will find his contribution rather disconcerting.

The critical historian can observe the fact of successive reinterpretations of the figure of the patriarch, and analyze their motives. He can also say what Abraham signified to successive generations and different religions. All of these things are historic phenomena, empirically controllable. But whether this pregnant vision of various traditions be conformable with the real, primitive, and human figure of the patriarch, cannot be guaranteed by the critical historian.

The author of biblical history operates with factors which, in part, are really adequate material for the writing of history. At the same time, however, he makes use of ultra-historical elements and transcendent causal agents which, as empirical evidence, could not be demonstrated.

The method of treating both kinds of factors is the same, because the biblical historiographer regards them as identical, with only one criterion of measurement. But this does not coincide with the literary style that is now called *history*. If the biblical narrator had known this style, he would not have accepted this label for what he had written.

For this reason, when the critical historian approaches the story of Abraham with the pure criteria of modern history, a conflict is then provoked. In this conflict the basis of all the interpretations is affected, so long as all of them claim to provide an historical version. How can this conflict be abated? Can critical history do justice to this other kind of history?

A few decades ago, critical history saw in the names of the patriarchs nothing more than imaginary heroes, tribal gods, or mythical characters. What was written in their name as history was merely a projection of the future of the people upon its past, thus explaining the social and religious situation which, at a given moment, had come to exist.

Today, new elements for the writing of history have entered the scene. Archeological findings in the Semitic world have illumined the whole era of the patriarchs of the Bible. In this newly revealed world, the names of persons, places, and peoples, the customs, institutions, and very movements of the patriarchs now appear normal, or at least highly probable.

This has produced a fresh current of historical optimism. But this optimism is a two-edged sword. It can serve to make the tradition of the patriarchs more comprehensible, as well as to deprive it of its function and empty it of meaning.

Archeological findings have made the historical existence of the patriarchs more probable, and have made possible the reconstruction of the environment and setting in which they lived. Doubtless, this is an acquisition of inestimable value. The basic historicity had always been the most reasonable supposition, the only one which made the traditions comprehensible. And this basic historicity now has in its favor the best guarantees that could be expected for such a remote era.

But these basic findings and this method do not really explain the tradition of the patriarchs. Anyone who tries to explain biblical history by enumerating the latest findings in Syria or Mesopotamia, in Phoenicia or Egypt, is in fact only preparing a setting for it. The historical setting of the era is all that archeology can help to construct. But the patriarchs move within it without any precision of time or place, without individual characteristics, and without certain guarantees of a personal existence. No doubt, many elements of biblical history are as ancient as the biblical historiographer claims to make them. But the patriarchs themselves are not more than probable figures, the chiefs of semi-nomadic clans marauding all over the region during the entire first three hundred years of the millennium.

The biblical tradition says much more about the patriarchs than a secular history of the same period could verify. Its author was not attempting to write the history of events as such, but to tell how his predecessors and contemporaries regarded them. Consequently, it is not the story itself that is important, but rather its interpretation. And to understand it, it is not sufficient to construct an external setting. It is necessary to interpret it as the historiographer did.

An objective reconstruction of events is not enough to make biblical history understandable. On the other hand, biblical history is not the guaranteed witness of events in the way that the latter may have occurred. Literary criticism continues to regard the traditions of the patriarchs as historically complex. Successive eras all had something to say about them. Various versions of the story adapted them to their general outlines. And it is well known that every version had its own tendencies and historiographical qualities, which attempt to reveal precisely and fittingly the historical origins, since this indicates a way and method for the history of following eras.

But in any of the various versions, pure history is merely a secondary factor.

The purpose of the author is to produce a theological history of the origins of the people. In this theological history, the most complex events are described as a simple occurrence, and the most heterogeneous relations are simplified in a genealogy. In a single action and moment, widely separated peoples and social groups come together, and different centuries are blended into one. Emigrations and displacements, undertaken by various nomadic groups in remote eras, from Mesopotamia to Palestine, and from Palestine to Egypt, appear as simple stages, accomplished all at once, by a compact group with a perfectly defined purpose. This simplification, however, covers a historical reality that is much more complex.

The Yahwist author, who wrote the first complete version of the story, was not anterior to the reign of David or Solomon. And this author wrote for his own era. The social, political, and religious environment in which he lived was his source of inspiration, and gave him the concrete sense and purpose of his story. But is this not, to some extent, the condition of the historian of all times and places?

There are real events which belong to the era described, but their interpretation belongs to the moment when they were written. Certainly, neither the Yahwist nor the other authors visualized their theological tendencies in findings of their imagination. All of the material was there before their eyes, in the popular traditions, whether oral or written. These traditions had found shelter in the warmth of a shrine or with a social group, and they had come down, in part, from the era of the patriarchs. Nevertheless, how many fluctuations there had been during such a long stretch of time!

These multiform traditions, which the historiographer integrates into a story, apparently organic, were previously separate. Different literary styles can be seen in them, including popular etymologies, etiological stories about caves, springs, trees and mountains, and family genealogies. In the traditions of Abraham there are elements of the cycle of Isaac and Jacob. In the most coherent traditions, Abraham is a man of the south, of Hebron and Mamre. He is the chief of a nomadic clan that lived in the region. His little story became the patrimony of the tribes which later came together in the south. Finally, when the tribes established themselves, the story of Abraham was of interest to all of them in common.[2]

The critical historian falters before this heterogeneity of elements, and if not by use of analogies, and at the cost of spending all his time reconstructing the social, political, and religious environment of the era, he gives up any attempt to reveal the real and human figure of Abraham. In the best of cases, what he finally reproduces is a common figure, like that of so many other nomads who lived in the same era and left no individual traces of their passage.

If the biblical narrator, using common material, succeeded in producing a figure like that of Abraham, it is because tradition had elaborated the material previously. The critical historian could not make use of it, elaborated in such a way, because it contains factors that resist the control of his criteria.

At times the modern critical historian is reproached for adopting an attitude towards religious history that is too negative. This reproach is perhaps justified. His attitude results from his commitment to treat history with the method of the natural sciences. In order to appear more objective, the historian tries to subject his materials to the process used in physics and botany, which requires observation, experiment, and induction. Anything that cannot be subjected to this process is eliminated, without further consideration.

However, to what point can this purism of methodology offer a refuge to the historian? In reality, can authentic history be satisfied with the analysis of a few depersonalized materials, and deny them the privilege of life, declaring itself powerless in life's

[2] See A. Weiser, "Abraham," in *RRG*, vol. I, pp. 63–71.

presence? To what point can the historian really attain, with the instruments of his art? There are moments when it becomes necessary to attempt the hard task of defining faculties and measuring forces. This occurs when the historian confronts religious history.

The historian knows very well that his materials, whether they be archeological remains, inscriptions, or documents, must be scrupulously verified. But he also knows that his task does not end with the collection and classification of materials. The bare facts, dissected and juxtaposed, are not called *history*. History must introduce the facts into the play of life. It can choose or discard, tear down or reconstruct, but it must bestow life. The historian must interpret the facts. There is no history without some form of interpretation.

But when it is interpreted, the conflict of *objectivity* arises at every step. Herein lies the drama: to interpret and be objective.

Absolute objectivity in history is, of course, a utopia. Nobody can attain it. No history, however comprehensive it may be, ever comprises all the aspects of reality. Modern history is accustomed to divide the fields into political or economic, military or religious. And though it does not lay claim to absolute objectivity, it can be accepted as relatively objective. But if it claimed more than this, it would not even be relatively so.

The writer of history, like his contemporaries, is the son of a particular civilization, an era and a nation. He cannot free himself from these limits, nor can his contemporaries, for whom the history is written, understand it unless it responds to their own exigencies. If, in spite of all, his history can be called objective, it is because of the relativity of the concept.

Pure objectivity could be claimed in the classification of plants or rocks or fossils, or in the external description of a physical phenomenon. But *man* is the material of history, and not dead man or a fossil, but living man, active in the midst of human society. And this makes a great difference.

This very complex being, which is man, and this complex

141

human society, labored by contradictory and indefinable forces, is the difficult and mysterious material which the historian must use in the writing of history. The external actions and the facts would be incomprehensible if the interior and living forces that cause them were not taken into account. But when can the historian subject these forces to analysis?

Man is not a mere *rational* thinker, who always makes use of logic. Nor did the men of history think of themselves and of things in the manner of modern man. The man of the past was not merely rational, and much less a rationalist. The man of today may be a rationalist, but he is not on that account more rational, nor is he necessarily more reasonable than his ancestors. This means that at no time can the historian relegate irrational forces to some dead area, as irrelevant factors of history.

If the historian is unable, whether empirically or logically, to subject them to control, they are not for that reason less real and effective. They are profound factors of history, because they are mysterious factors of complex human nature.

If it were necessary to eliminate from the biblical history of the patriarchs everything which reason or experience does not control, and all that the author expresses in ingenuous form, there would not be any meaning in this history at all. To decompose the traditions into their simple and primitive elements is like decomposing a poem or a symphony. Anecdotes, sayings, or notes out of context are dead material. Only the artist who interprets and intuits could restore meaning to them.

This is the field of uncertain boundaries and shifting sand in which the historian operates. This is his drama. To run away from it because of its difficulty, and take refuge in certitude, is to declare himself unfaithful to the task.

The critical historian, however, has his limits. No one can compel him to go beyond them. Anyone who does not recognize in history anything more than immanent and intra-mundane factors, cannot adequately cope with the biblical history of the patriarchs. The figure of Abraham, as the biblical narrator presents him, would not be conformable with the rules of modern history, and even less with those of profane history. It might be possible to write a history of his history, but all the factors could not be subjected to the criteria of history.

In modern terms, the tradition of Abraham is much more than a historical narrative. It is a theology and a pedagogy, or a *theological pedagogy*. Within a framework of historical aspect, it is the formulation of a *credo*.

Insofar as this tradition has the framework of history, there are political, social, and economic aspects. It witnesses to the customs and institutions of the era. It includes deeds and feats of biographical character. But all of this is simply the framework and setting. The real content is the past (in this case the pre-history of the people visualized in Abraham), as the field of action of a superior agent.

There is here a conflict between two kinds of history: profane history, which is *immanent,* and biblical history, which is *theological.* But this conflict is wholly unnecessary, because they are different kinds of history, each having its own methods and means. If neither of them exceeds its own limits, the clash does not occur.

The same story of Abraham can be reached by various approaches and from different points of departure. There are distinct methods to approach truth, and truth itself has many aspects. This is the case with the story of Abraham, as soon as reason has separated the world of faith from the world of science.

All of the fields that were once the exclusive domain of the *theological method* have been invaded by the *scientific method.* The very object that had always merited the believer's respect was finally opened to the implacable analysis of the critic. There are two different roads leading to the same goal. And the same goal must finally be divided in order to satisfy those who, following different roads, lay claim to it. Obviously, everyone reaching it sees it only from his own point of view. And perhaps two persons see things that are different or even contradictory, which cannot be mutually tolerated. But how could both observers ever agree? Are they not both looking at things from sides that are opposed?

The biblical narrator sees in the traditional stories of the patriarch a divine plan and a divine event. Everything that occurs is governed by an extra-mundane agent. There is nothing "secular" which could escape this control. The entire story has an organic meaning and purpose, which Yahweh determines, indicating to Abraham a particular road with a clear goal. Everything is accomplished purposefully, and everything moves towards that goal. When the temporal promises had been ful- filled, the end had not yet been reached. Once the land was possessed, all the action was then concentrated on keeping it, or in acquiring it again when it was lost. When the chosen people one day had to abandon their land, the prophetic and eschatolog- ical visions stressed the promises of the land and opened new roads, so that the story would never lack significance. The story of Abraham is one stage in this long road of providence.

The immanent method seeks only the human and rational side of the events. For the biblical narrator they are all symbols of divine action. Neither the existence of God nor the reality of His action needs to be demonstrated, for He is the fount and source. For the one who creates, everything is demonstration, and for the one who does not create, no demonstration is sufficient. The one who creates sees the action of God, even in things that can be explained by human or natural causality. Every event in his- tory and every phenomenon of nature speaks the language of a divine message. Every form of reality is an image, a symbol, which arose spontaneously and which tradition has consecrated. And every image or symbol speaks directly of the divine action.

If the biblical narrator had to make his own criticism, he would say that his approach is a normal process which does not claim to be adequate to the transcendent object. He simply turns towards it and aims for it. The facts of history are not important

merely because they occurred or never occurred. Their importance is in being symbols, and being able, as such, to express
what would otherwise be inexpressible.

The story of Abraham substantiates in visible happenings a
sure theology, perfectly defined. It is never set forth in theoretical
formulas, but always in visible forms. The reader will search in
vain for explicit theological formulas or judgments, like those
given in Deuteronomy. One cannot even see its theological framework, nor is its connection with the context of the story ever
visualized in concrete formulas. The relation with the context
can be found in the formulas of connection in the various
episodes.[3] However, the relation with the context is more
definitely found in the spirit of the story.

If an express and condensed formula of connection of this
story with the story that follows after is desired, it will be found
in the professions of faith of the patriarch's descendants.

And you shall make response before the Lord your God, "A wandering Aramean was my father; and he went down into Egypt and sojourned there, few in number; and there he became a nation, great,
mighty, and populous."[4]

The story of the patriarch is summed up in this formula of faith,
which expressly relates it with all the rest of the history.

History and theology meet in the traditions of Abraham,
perfectly united, inseparable and indistinct. History is subordinate
to theology, and acclimated to it. Even if the facts and events
had been more complex, or had been different, theological truth
hovered over them, like an exquisite perfume in a vase of clay.

The conflict of the immanent and theological methods in deal-
ing with the story of Abraham would never occur if each would
hold strictly to its own procedures. The immanent method would
make the effort to reach its objective, putting into play all the
instruments of its art. And once it had reached its own Abraham,
it would neither affirm nor deny ultimate realities which lie

[3] See Gen. 12:1–9; 18:17–19.   [4] Deut. 26:5.

beyond its scope. Can there not be another point of view from which many other dimensions of the story are visible?

On the other hand, however, the theological method should not attempt to justify itself by resorting to immanent procedures. The contributions of archeology, even if they were greatly multiplied, would never explain the biblical figure of Abraham. It is said that the history of salvation must be wholly explained in terms of spectacular interventions of God in time, or rather at precise times. If immanent history, in its own way, guarantees the reality of these interventions (for example, by assuring the historicity of Abraham), the illusion is held that now everything is quite evident. After each spectacular intervention, Abraham would have lived in inactivity, simply waiting for another spectacular experience.

As a matter of fact, this conception finds support in the general scheme and outline of biblical history. That is why there must be an absolute acceptance of everything it sets forth as factual. And there can be no doubt that there were events in the past that made an impression. Without them, not even this general outline could be explained. But if the real nature of history is taken into account, it cannot be said that the intervals were inactive. On the contrary, it was during the intervals that the events were carefully considered and understood in their spectacular and salvific dimension. This way of understanding history, seeing in each occurrence a divine event, is the work of uninterrupted reflection. It is not the work of a day. What tradition presents as a fact is not merely a fact. It is a visual picture, to which the religious mind has added the colors of its faith.

Pure history does not attempt to verify events of such proportions. But neither were the events originally clothed with the certain significance that accompanies them today. The soteriological activity of God is permanent. The religious consciousness "understands" and experiences it step by step, and formulates it in some way or other, by symbolizing it in facts and events. Without the gradual awakening of religious consciousness, and

146

without the continuous purification of the theological conception, the same facts would never precisely state their meaning or deliver their message. The facts of history are always bare at the start, like the birth of any poor creature. And they remain bare unless a familiar hand gives them shelter.

The facts of history, even at their origin, can be the cause of a very decisive experience. But the assimilation of this experience and its functional interpretation are not the work of a day. With the passing of time, the pure facts are enlarged or simplified, consolidated or changed, thus acquiring, in a word, their difinitive value.

It is not strange that the historian refuses to attempt to verify them, for in reality their form is constantly changing. Every new reflection modifies them. Every new interpretation enlarges them, making them the foundation-stone of a whole new edifice. And even then their career has not ended, for they point to the future, and to new constructions, and worlds of another shape, with other ideas. Finally, it is not the facts that matter, but the message they contain.

Since there are different ways to approach the facts of history, the language used is also different. The story of Abraham speaks in one way to the person seeking only the comprehensible and explicable, rejecting whatever fails to accord with reason, and in another way to the person who is willing to accept and engage himself in the internal logic of the writer of the story. Abraham interests both the *rationalist* and the *believer,* but from different points of view.

The rationalist seeks the pure facts in the story. The believer wants to know what they signify, or what the historiographer wanted to say in them. The same facts are merely materials of an intramundane story for the one, whereas for the other they are symbols of divine action. The former asks what they contain for historical purposes; the latter wants to know their significance for consequent activity. According to the rationalist, Abraham is an archaic figure, clothed in his legend with mythical garb.

147

For the believer, however, he is a living figure, the sign of a message of God that continues to the present day.

The rationalist and believer speculate upon different bases and with different values. While the rationalist considers as illusory what the other esteems in the patriarch, the believer rejects the limitations of the rationalist. Both realize that the author of the story saw transcendent factors operative in it. Both of them also know what this signifies, since they are religious factors, and the latter are universally human. But it is one thing to know the phenomenon of religious belief, and quite another actually to believe. It is one thing to know what others say about the divine factor, and something else to recognize its operation in the course of history.

If neither went beyond his own limits, there would be no conflict. But on the field of battle no agreement is possible, since both are radically opposed from their very point of departure. The rationalist would not accept a compromise, which would be the denial of his own nature. The believer who calls himself a "liberal" will attempt to compromise, each time yielding a little of what may seem unessential for his purpose. However, there is no assurance that by making concessions he will reach an agreement, because the exigencies of the rationalist do not decrease, and the reason for yielding, once the process begins, has no limits. In the position of a believer, the "integrist" is more logical than the "liberal," for with regard to the object of faith, he is not concerned with distinctions between the essential and the secondary. It is rather a matter of position and methods. For anyone maintaining this position, there is no real difference between the essential and the secondary. And for the believer whose position inclines him to make concessions, there will never be a better reason for proceeding slowly. No agreement is possible between the believer and the rationalist. But neither is there any good reason for continuing this battle. If neither goes beyond his own limits, there can be no conflict.

The biblical story of Abraham necessarily rejects every kind of rationalist interpretation. From the moment that the patriarch heard the call of Yahweh and followed it, he was no longer merely a natural man, following his reason and his instincts. Nor was he the simple Bedouin, seeking bread and posterity. However ardently he sought these things, both were a symbol of ulterior realities. And the roads he traveled in seeking them were not usual either.

If Abraham had followed only his natural lights, he would not have abandoned his native land in such circumstances, and certainly he would not have gone to Moriah. But once he had heard the command of Yahweh, the only "reasonable" thing to do, contrary to all reason, was to follow trustingly, whatever the consequences might be.

For the writer of the story, the patriarch followed the only "reasonable" course. And even more than reasonable, it was the only sure and safe course, since it was Yahweh Himself who would provide. It did not matter, therefore, that the goal seemed impossible and humanly absurd. The God who promised was also capable of making it attainable, if the patriarch responded. The risk of obeying was very small compared with the risk of traveling alone, with impossible things to overcome on the way.

Abraham did everything with peace of mind and traveled without any feeling of tragedy. Even when he climbed Moriah. He felt neither anguish nor despair, for the certain "logic" of his course spared him any tragic presentiment. And it is this unshakable certitude and security that cannot be accepted or understood unless one has had some part in it. The believer who walks with Abraham understands it. But not the rationalist, who cannot see how that course can be logical.

Abraham does not appear in his story with any human or personal weakness, because he is an ideal and its symbol. In a historical body there is a soul of theological design. Abraham was a just man, and the faith of his people has taken him for a guide. He is not only what he was, but what they have made of him by their interpretation. For that reason, when he encountered the

149

Numinous, there was no shiver of fear in him, but only a peaceful attraction. If he had been "humanized" again, he would have lost his function as a symbol.

To understand the story of Abraham in its profound reality, it is not, therefore, the human datum that really matters, but the "logic" that peacefully governed his life. To remove myth from tradition is to make the latter pure history, at the cost of depriving it of what is really important. That is why the believer cannot make concessions to the rationalist who, for his part, cedes nothing either. To make concessions is to enter into the rational artfulness of the adversary, abandoning an impregnable position, and, when conquered, giving up one's own stronghold.

Consequently, the tradition of Abraham has but little value for a history that is merely immanent. Its value is *religious*. Abraham is of interest to the world as a religious figure. Only this aspect has been able to surpass the distances of space and time.

But the gift of survival, even with regard to this aspect, still has conditions. After many centuries, the figure of Abraham lived again in the days of the Yahwist author, at the cost of an *adaptation* to the demands of his era. And it continued to live on by adaptation, always being adapted in order to continue living. This does not mean that his figure has changed, or that his message has been altered. It is rather the living generations which change, and which must make the adaptation in order to make the figure of Abraham present.

Every kind of history, including the secular and critical, is meant to perform a function in the society of the one who writes it. All history is "contemporary" when it is being written. Even when the events are remote by thousands of years, the social, religious, and cultural present of the historian vibrates in the facts and events which he relates and interprets. The remote past, when evoked again, enjoys a vital solidarity with the present, like a guest invited to take part. If it were not for this, there would be no reason to evoke it. But as soon as it lives anew, it

150

stimulates the present like an ancient of days who had never died.

That is why all history, every so often, must be interpreted again. Those who in times past made their interpretation, did so for themselves, from their own point of view. Each day requires its own message. The subjective version is always inseparable from history if the latter is to have any significance. Absolute objectivity is not altered by this, however, because it is only partially attainable, according to the exact measure of the subject. Israel and Moab waged war together. The book of Kings and the stele of Mesha both tell of it. And referring to the same events, each of these sources related a victory for its own side. Abraham, in the Bible, is the father of a numerous posterity. The sons of Israel and the sons of Hagar understand this in an ethnic sense, and all of them call him father. St. Paul understood it in a spiritual sense, and made him the father of all believers.

"Man," as Croce would say, "is a microcosm, not in the natural sense, but in an historical sense. He is a compendium of universal history." This means that every era somehow receives the fruits of the past, or that the latter continues to live in the present. If it were not for this shortening of distances, we could not absolutely know the past, for we are unable to know anything that is wholly alien to us. However, once it has been brought into convenient nearness to us, the past helps us to know the present, which is too close to ourselves to see it clearly.

In religious history the process is the same. If the figure of Abraham had not been *actualized,* it would not be understandable in our time, or would not be important. Abraham would be nothing more than the ambitious nomad of secular history, or the anachronic figure of legend, or a great symbolical personage of interest to his own ethnic group exclusively. He could not have helped us to understand ourselves, nor could we formulate our own activity through his experience.

His story is continually open, and can be read and understood again and again. His descendants have been reading it down

151

through the ages and are still doing so, including both his carnal descendants and those who are newcomers to his inheritance.

Even as yesterday, men of our time turn to the patriarch. His message is not yet exhausted or closed. It has not been definitively delivered. Whatever is born of time is enduring, unless it be perishable. And the Abraham of the rationalist is the only Abraham that has perished. The other does not perish because he is renewed every day in the experience and requirements of the believer. This is the dimension that makes the patriarch comprehensible and helps us to understand our present existence.

To *actualize* is the magic word. Because to actualize is to keep the past alive and let ourselves be illumined by its wisdom. The effect, however, does not obtain when an inert attitude is adopted towards the past, except by laborious effort. It is not the one that plagiarizes a model who makes the latter live, but rather the one who imitates him. The one enchains him to his past, and the other rejuvenates him. Actualization does not destroy the identity of the thing or person actualized. The future of an enterprise belongs to the enterprise, and the future of a person belongs to the person, the same as the past. The future of an event, and its interpretation, also belong to the original event. Abraham does not cease to exist while he lives in his descendants. Nor does he lose his identity when his descendants interpret him. In the latest interpretations, he may have reached a serene maturity and mellowness which he could not possess in the first one.

The Yahwist author, in formulating the first interpretation which tradition made of the patriarch, ascribed an historical setting to him which has also served for subsequent interpretations. The visual setting is necessary for the plasticity of the pedagogy. Without it, neither the permanent message nor the temporary message could have taken root in existence. The patriarch, in this setting, is found to be sufficiently like a personal and human figure to serve as a visible symbol, and sufficiently unlike it to ensure the agility of his message.

His human likeness and nearness could be emphasized, and

this is what pure history would do. In the light of what is known about the era, a rationally comprehensible figure of Abraham could now be produced. However, neither archeology nor comparative history can illumine more than his human figure. But if that is all, there is no message to be found in the story of the patriarch. On the other hand, the denial or rejection of the entire human setting would destroy the visual medium and would make the message purely theoretical. The visual setting and the agility of a proportionate remoteness are both necessary at the same time.

Anyone who perceives a living figure in Abraham is already interpreting him in terms of his own interest and capacity. What once belonged entirely to one people becomes the heritage of all nations. What was said about him long ago is repeated in new language. A call and message of Yahweh can also be expressed by silent inspiration; His apparition by inward awareness. The journey to Moriah and the raising of the knife also have real and intelligible correspondence in a thousand other acts of renunciation in the life of a believer. What cannot be done is to anchor the figure of Abraham in the past. The passing of time is not in vain. There are things of the past that are lost beyond redemption. Either they cannot be recovered, although this may be desired, or they would be repugnant in their ancient form to the eyes of the present.

The elimination of myth is fashionable among those who are concerned with ancient religious history. If this means the elimination of irrational or super-rational factors from the documents of the past, it is obvious that its result is an immanent, intramundane history. And this is not necessarily the only objective.

But to "demythologize" can also be a translation into modern, understandable terminology, without attempting or claiming to eliminate the factors that cannot be subjected to analysis, or which transcend rational knowledge. If the suppression of these factors were required, the religious history of the past would be

153

converted into a field of dry bones. And who is the prophet that would bend over them to infuse them with new life?

The story of Abraham would be dead without the irrational and transcendent factor. In order to actualize it, it must be alive, with a God who commands and a patriarch who sets out upon his journeys, imbued with hope.

It is not difficult to eliminate the mythical, nor is it difficult to say that the patriarch's journeys were absurd. The difficulty lies in still finding significance in the story of Abraham and in the history of his descendants. If the validity of the religious meaning is not acknowledged, no philosophical reasoning will find any significance in it.

The story of Abraham is not immanent history. Its domain is on the margin of pure history. Its character and concrete limits are not easily defined, for neither is it easy to define the limits of history as a science. Rational verification of the facts by empirical methods is the basic criterion of pure history, but it is not easy to use and apply this criterion uniformly.

It is more feasible to indicate the limits of empirical verification. Philosophical reasoning goes beyond it, still pursuing the object, when empirical methods have lost touch with it. This pursuit finally extends to the margin of the science of history. But philosophical reasoning, in its turn, also has its limits. These are even more difficult to define, for it would be necessary to be greater than man and external to him in order adequately to measure a human faculty. Modern psychology recognizes in man the importance of the depths of the unconscious and other capacities which rationalism had systematically rejected. With this development, the mystery of man has become more profound, and the definition of his limits more difficult. But the limits do exist, they are imposed by the object.

In the field of knowledge, the believer ventures towards distances and objects which no natural faculty could reach. Not that the believer understands them, but he intuits them, so to speak. Nor does he quite embrace them, but rather feels them, as though within reach of the hand. In this area reason would not encounter the process of cause and effect. Imagination would not find images sufficiently expressive. But the boldness of faith, as a strange human faculty, successfully contacts this unlimited domain which eye has not seen, nor ear heard, nor any human sense perceived. It is only with symbols and analogies that it is possible, in some way, to speak of this mysterious domain.

This is, therefore, the field of knowledge which the natural faculties are unable to penetrate, and in which no kind of empirical analysis is applicable. It is a field that is completely on the margin of the immanent criteria of history. But this is the field in which the first one to write the story of the patriarch was operative, as well as all the others who subsequently interpreted him.

The objective reality of everything in the story that is pre-supposed, is something that cannot be demonstrated, because to demonstrate is to call into play a human faculty with a capacity to understand. But neither can it be rejected, because in order to do this one must first know it and consider it worthless. In the simple human order, undemonstrable realities are more numerous than those which, in fact, can be demonstrated. And this is not a sufficient reason to exclude them from the order of existent things.

The limitation of natural man is quite notorious. Anyone who at some time or other has claimed to go beyond it, has run up against the barrier that cannot be overcome. Both science and philosophy, or any form of human knowledge, all have the cruel capacity to lead man to the heights, only to give him a taste of the deepest humiliation.

Human reason has so much experience and practice in having to be humbled before itself and before little things, that it ought to be able to be humble before the incomprehensible logic of the story of Abraham. If it could not do this, its road would be closed within a very short distance. Neither the longing to live, nor the privilege of knowing, nor the awareness of being something distinct from other creatures of this world, would have any significance in man. If there is no more reality than can be known empirically or rationally, there is neither a goal nor sufficient significance for history as a whole, nor for the individual either.[5] The incomprehensible "logic" of the patriarch keeps open the roads towards a meaningful goal. And he leaves this same meaningful goal as a legacy to all believers.

The story of Abraham is a theme of salutary meditation for the person who lives sheltered within the castle of his natural lights. But neither could it be without importance to anyone who habitually reasons with the logic of faith.

The habit of living by religious experience of the past, as is the case with the believer, moderates personal activity in a great and purposeful undertaking that directly concerns the person. Past experiences are converted into a formula, and the formula is more schematic than life-like. It purifies experience of personal aims and interests, transforming it into a common good, accessible to all. However, in its universal capacity, this experience would serve no purpose if it did not come alive again in the person, letting itself be adopted as his own experience.

To prevent the death of the formula, it may perhaps be necessary to immerse it again in the water of its source and fount, so that it may be infused with new life. If its own vitality is not sufficient, we may have to turn our eyes to Abraham and observe how this experience was realized in him. Abraham is a model, and he accomplishes everything in his quiet way. But possibly in walking beside him we will feel in ourselves the creaking and trembling that shake our whole being when we encounter the Eternal.

[5] I do not believe that there is any reason to reject as "mythical" the significance and goal of history as a whole, in order to admit them in the individual. Or to suppress universal eschatology, in order to replace it by a personal kind, realized at every moment on the basis of personal decisions. Reason would have the same difficulty admitting a real and transcendent goal for the individual as for history. But faith can admit it for both with the same facility. (Allusion to R. Bultmann, *History and Eschatology*, New York, 1962.)

The encounter with God is not always so simple. When it takes place, almost always at the outer edge of human experience, it can bring about dreadful consequences. Sometimes it pleases God to lead us along strange roads and ways that our natural lights cannot reach. And the person who experiences the encounter begins to "reason" with a distinct kind of logic that is not always on peaceful terms with normal logic.

But it is salutary to have this experience for oneself, going beyond the formula, and feeling and living it in the moment that the shock of encounter occurs.

Every so often we must listen anew to the stories of the patriarch. His message has been proclaimed many times, but only for the moment that was passing. It must be proclaimed again, as was done by our predecessors. The patriarch would, at various times, have listened to the voice again. Even though the voice is the same, all of us must listen personally. What was said to the patriarch for everyone, must be heard by each of us for himself: Go from your country . . . Journey forth upon these roads . . . Renounce the descendant of the slave woman . . . Climb up Moriah . . . and finally, I shall make you the possessor of my promises.

CARMELITE MONASTERY
Beckley Hill
Barre, Vt., 05641

DATE BORROWED